"In this engagingly written book, Meghar
new hope for the cause of the gospel. Anc
addressing my fears—and even by correct
cal confusions!"

RICHARD J. MOUW, president emeritus and senior professor of faith and
public life at Fuller Seminary

"I'm so grateful for gifted leaders like Meghan Larissa Good who are
not only theologizing about ways forward for Christian leaders and
communities but also experimenting with embodying creative theology
in congregational practice. The world needs to see congregations of
people who are actually following Christ, and that's exactly where
Divine Gravity leads."

BRIAN D. MCLAREN, author of *Do I Stay Christian?*

"Though it is still far off most people's radar screen, there is a grass-
roots movement of the Spirit around the globe in which individuals
and groups are rediscovering the beauty of a Jesus-centered God who
empowers them to live like Jesus in order to partner with God in
transforming our world in a Jesus-kind-of-way. With this powerful
and insightful book, Meghan Larissa Good gives voice to this rising
movement, highlighting its distinctive convictions while addressing
how it corrects distortions of the gospel in the past. In the process, she
presents a vision of God, the church, and the world that is as refreshing
as it is compelling. If you're one of the many who have lost hope in
the church, or who just got bored, you owe it to yourself to read this
remarkable book!"

GREGORY A. BOYD, senior pastor of Woodland Hills Church in Maplewood,
Minnesota, president of ReKnew Ministries (ReKnew.org), and author of
Cross Vision

"With *Divine Gravity*, pastor Meghan Larissa Good has created a
work that will make followers of Jesus rethink what faith and faithfulness mean in the twenty-first century. Her work is thought-provoking,
deeply scriptural, and delightfully cheeky. Readers may not agree with
Good on every count, but the questions she poses are invaluable for we
who collectively and desperately desire a realignment of the Western
church to God's great story."

ONEYA OKUWOBI, teaching pastor at 21st Century Church and assistant
professor of sociology at University of Cincinnati

"*Divine Gravity* offers a vividly written, hugely relevant, Anabaptist-inflected presentation of the way of Jesus. Meghan Larissa Good is clearly a rising star of the next generation of Christian writers. I will be looking forward to hearing what she has to say for many years to come."

DAVID P. GUSHEE, Distinguished University Professor of Christian Ethics and director of the Center for Theology and Public Life at Mercer University and author of *After Evangelicalism*

"*Much is wrong with Christianity, and Jesus is the answer.* Meghan Larissa Good breathes new life into that tired phrase. In this book, doubters, critics, and the wounded will feel heard. She acknowledges the depth of the problems. She presses beyond cliché and shallow understandings of Jesus and sparks hope. The way of Jesus that she presents truly can bring change. This book overflows with images, stories, and illustrations that communicate deep insights with freshness and clarity."

MARK D. BAKER, professor of Mission and Theology at Fresno Pacific Biblical Seminary and author of *Centered-Set Church*

"As the twenty-first-century church has wandered from its center and lost track of Jesus, this book can help us rediscover and return to the centrality of Jesus—or, I should say, this book can help reorient us toward Jesus again. *Divine Gravity* is so timely—it gives us fresh air to breathe, an air of hope that shows the Spirit is at work stirring something again. What the Protestant Reformation did in the sixteenth century, *Divine Gravity* might do for us today, ushering us into a rediscovery of Jesus and his centrality to the Christian faith and life."

SAMUEL KEFAS SARPIYA, executive director at the Center for Nonviolence and Conflict Transformation in Rockford, Illinois

"A timely book indeed! In a world increasingly running short on hope, and with a keen and piercing analysis of our time, Meghan Larissa Good dares to hope! Her hope is based on an alternative story to that of the world, which is that God is at work renewing all things. God's redemptive work might seem distant and untenable to many which is why now is the time to re-story the Christian story. Good provides the reason why we should do this and the resources to employ to recover that better story. This book is a must-read for those who believe in the story of Jesus and dare to hope for a better, God-shaped future for creation."

NELSON OKANYA, Global Missions President of the Center for Serving Leadership and chair of Global Mission Fellowship for Mennonite World Conference

divine
gravity

MEGHAN LARISSA GOOD

divine gravity

SPARKING A MOVEMENT TO RECOVER A BETTER CHRISTIAN STORY

HERALD PRESS

Harrisonburg, Virginia

Herald Press
PO Box 866, Harrisonburg, Virginia 22803
www.HeraldPress.com

Library of Congress Cataloging-in-Publication Data
Names: Good, Meghan Larissa, author.
Title: Divine gravity : sparking a movement to recover a better Christian
     story / Meghan Larissa Good.
Description: Harrisonburg, Virginia : Herald Press, [2023] | Includes
     bibliographical references.
Identifiers: LCCN 2023024664 (print) | LCCN 2023024665 (ebook) | ISBN
     9781513813127 (paperback) | ISBN 9781513813134 (hardcover) | ISBN
     9781513813141 (ebook)
Subjects: LCSH: Church renewal--History. | Church history. | Christian
     life. | BISAC: RELIGION / Christian Living / Spiritual Growth | RELIGION
     / Christian Church / General
Classification: LCC BV600.3 .G662 2023 (print) | LCC BV600.3 (ebook) |
     DDC 262.001/7--dc23/eng/20230710
LC record available at https://lccn.loc.gov/2023024664
LC ebook record available at https://lccn.loc.gov/2023024665

Produced in partnership with

ⓙ Jesus Collective

Study guides are available for many Herald Press titles at www.HeraldPress.com.

DIVINE GRAVITY
© 2023 by Herald Press, Harrisonburg, Virginia 22803. 800-245-7894.
     All rights reserved.
Library of Congress Control Number: 2023024664
International Standard Book Number: 978–1-5138-1312-7 (paperback);
     978-1-5138-1313-4 (hardcover); 978-1-5138-1314-1 (ebook)
Printed in United States of America

27 26 25 24 23   10 9 8 7 6 5 4 3 2 1

*To Trinity Mennonite Church and Albany
Mennonite Church,*
   *who have embraced the messy experiment of
life together as "future people"*

And to Scott,
   *who challenged my faith and helped me see
Jesus more clearly*

Contents

Foreword

In 1985, I started working as a custodian in a church until I left for seminary the next year. Then, in 1987, I began working part-time on the ministerial staff at a church, and I went on to work in some full-time pastoral role or another until 2018, when I became a full-time New Testament seminary instructor. I've worked for churches for over thirty years, and I've also taught the Bible (either as an adjunct professor or full-time instructor) for over twenty years (yes, sometimes my teaching and pastoral roles overlapped). And prior to getting financial compensation for my work in churches, I was an active member—volunteering to serve in numerous ways. I share these words about my church background to point out that I have been more than a casual observer of Christianity in the USA. I have been an active participant, paying attention to the trends, the fads, the celebrities, and the abuses. There are times when I beam with pride over how godly people demonstrate the Jesus way of life in ordinary as well as complex situations. But there are also times when I cringe because self-proclaimed Christians engaged in evil actions and perpetuated injustices. It's fair to say that for some of us, being called "Christian" can be embarrassing.

Meghan Good has also paid attention to how Christianity has operated in our society and imagines a renewal—a reformation. Meghan is a pastor who has not just read statistics or books about societal trends but has ministered with people who are striving to navigate life in our complex society. Meghan knows how a segment of our society feels because she shares those feelings. And in her sharing of life with others, Meghan has come to see that there can be a better way. She writes not as an all-knowing expert who tells us how to live our most successful life, or who can give us the "seven secrets to building a better church." Instead, Meghan explores key points of tension, such as how we approach the Bible, how we communicate the good news of Jesus Christ, and how we engage in work, power, and interpersonal conflict. Meghan's insights are not those of an authoritarian telling us what to do and be, but are words from a friend inviting us to dream about how things can be better, to imagine how we can know abundant, meaningful life (see John 10:10)—even within a complex, pluralistic, violent, and often confusing world.

For example, Meghan's assertion that salvation is meant to be "a comprehensive rescue of humanity and all creation from everything that distorts its design" (p. 68) is refreshing to me, as I've often witnessed people defining salvation as some sort of spiritual transaction that might have little or no consequence for life on earth. At various points I didn't merely nod in agreement with Meghan's words, but felt I was being invited to resist cynicism and renew my hope that "Christian" need not spark embarrassment but excitement. Of course, it is Jesus who is the reason for the excitement, and Meghan reminds us that Jesus is the center of our story.

In the first century, a few years after Jesus had been raised from the dead and the Holy Spirit was poured out on the first groups of believers, the word *Christian* was used as an insult tossed at some Jesus followers. I imagine some of those early believers had complicated feelings when they were called "Christian." Some likely felt shame at the designation. In fact, the apostle Peter encourages his readers by saying, "But don't be ashamed if you suffer as one who belongs to Christ. Rather, honor God as you bear Christ's name. Give honor to God" (1 Peter 4:16). These early followers of Jesus—living in world that emphasized honor and expended great energy to avoid shame—needed to understand that *Christian* might not be well understood by everyone, but nevertheless signified hope. Peter wrote that faith in Jesus provided "a living hope" (1 Peter 1:3). Hope is possible because Jesus saves—salvation for life now and for the life yet to come.

Gravity can be defined as a force that attracts a body toward the center. *Divine Gravity* invites us all to experience the attractional tug of life with Jesus at the center.

—Dennis R. Edwards
Dean, North Park Theological Seminary

Introduction

Are We Living through a New Reformation?

One day in the fall of 1995, a section of cliff broke off Multnomah Falls, the second-highest waterfall in the United States. A rock slab roughly the size of a school bus plummeted 150 feet, hurling water and debris hundreds of feet into the air and damaging the bridge on which a shocked wedding party stood taking pictures 100 feet above the ground.

The terrifying event caught everyone off guard. According to witnesses, the only warning was the sound of a sharp crack. But of course, multi-ton boulders don't just suddenly tear themselves away from cliffs. The freeze-thaw cycle had been slowly expanding fissures unnoticed, probably for years, before the impact became abruptly visible. Pebble by loosened pebble, there simply came a tipping point when the force pulling down was greater than the forces holding things in place.

Something about this scene may feel uncannily familiar to recent observers of Christianity in the West. Seasons come and go, but the basic landscape is unchanged. And then seemingly from nowhere, in the middle of the normal business of marrying and burying and fighting about carpet, all hell suddenly breaks loose. Institutions, traditions, doctrines, social norms, and ways of life that just yesterday seemed immovable are cracking, plummeting. In the hail of debris, it's hard to comprehend the scale of the breakage, let alone process causes or long-term effects.

WHAT SPARKED THE LAST REFORMATION

Five hundred years ago, a priest named Martin Luther published a list of ninety-five "theses" (theological propositions) that helped touch off a cascade of change across the Western world. Luther's actions did not "cause" any of the world-reshaping developments that followed any more than the shift of one stone remade a whole cliff-face. The forces applying pressure, creating cracks, had been in play for decades. Neither was Luther a radical theological innovator setting out to intentionally ignite revolution. He saw himself as simply calling the church back into alignment with its historical faith.

Yet the impact of this rediscovery of the Christian foundations was cataclysmic. Long-widening fissures and a multitude of shifting pebbles finally reached a tipping point. The resulting cascade leveled established hierarchies and traditions and redrew the landscape of both church and nations for centuries afterward.

One of the fissures that made the sixteenth-century world ripe for revolution was widespread abuse of religious power, most infamously displayed in the sale of indulgences. Cancellation of sin could be purchased with the currencies of good deeds, service in war, or most convenient for those who could afford it, a generous financial donation. A skilled preacher could drive up demand by seasoning his sermon with strategic pyrotechnics— just a little taste of brimstone to remind you what you're risking by not locking in forgiveness with this limited-time offer.

General confusion surrounding religious authority also contributed to the growing pressure. Multiple popes and religious councils competed for preeminence, raising the obvious question of whom God was truly backing. Meanwhile, schools of biblical scholarship that had sprung up in the Middle Ages challenged the shaky interpretative grounds on which many established church traditions rested. It turned out the church had valued customs for which it could no longer marshal a convincing explanation. We twenty-first-century people might recognize the feeling. If anyone's checking, Jesus never actually said, "Thou shalt celebrate my defeat of death each spring by gorging on chocolate rabbits and marshmallow chickens."

In addition, in the sixteenth century, not for the first or last time, gaps were widening between the formal theology of the church and religious ideas popularized among ordinary people. The Catholic Church, for example, had never held that salvation could be earned with good works. Yet somehow, many lay Christians remained under the impression that God's approval might be won—or lost—on the basis of personal performance.

The ground-shifts that set the stage for the Protestant Reformation were not all internal to the church. Just as important were larger changes in culture and technology. The sixteenth-century reformation likely would not have unfolded at such a large scale without the invention of the printing press decades earlier. As this new technology became widely adopted, ideas could disseminate with unprecedented speed. And more and more people could read for themselves. No longer was everyone willing to take the village priest's word for it. Church hierarchies had to compete in a rapidly expanding public marketplace of ideas.

This was the moment when Martin Luther put forth for public conversation his theses addressing where the church had gotten off course and required recalibration. On its own, it was just a spark, an act of frustrated complaint not uncommon among scholars in any field or century. But this spark struck a church littered with dry kindling, igniting a world-reshaping forest fire.

Ultimately, the spiritual energy that drove the Protestant Reformation might be boiled down to a few key ideas: The Bible—not any individual, institution, or tradition—is the anchor for Christian authority. Christ's grace is an unmerited gift no one can buy, sell, or control. Faith, not religious performance, makes one right with God.

None of these were exactly innovative notions. They were fresh articulations of ancient Christian truths. But their rediscovery unleashed an explosion of energy and reframed how generations since have understood and practiced Christianity, for both good and ill. This was true not only for the Protestant Reformers who left their previous institutions to start new communities but also for many who stayed within the Catholic Church and ultimately undertook their own important internal reforms.

A REFORMATION'S PURPOSE

Reformation periods are by nature disruptive, tumultuous, and unsettling. In the worst cases, they can become profoundly divisive and even violent. Yet from its earliest days, the Christian movement has also emphasized the necessity of regular rhythms of repentance. This, you might say, is reformation at its best. A reformation movement is a repentance movement, a regularly required period of communal reflection and reorientation.

Even individual humans, who live just decades, experience the occasional need to recalibrate, reclaim their true identity, go back and pick up things they left behind. The Christian church has been around for more than two thousand years. Drift happens. Small navigational errors compound over time. Customs outlast memory of their purpose. Experiments are conducted and theories are tested over generations, and the results aren't always predictable.

A reformation is not about reinventing religion. It isn't a revelation of ideas no one has conceived of before. A reformation is a period of course-correction. It is marked by a return to core truths and an untangling of misapprehensions. It involves a removal of plaque that builds up over time and a pruning of false growth produced by widespread cultural distortions.

The decades after Luther's publication are often called "*the* Reformation," but these events are not as singular as the name seems to imply. They cannot be. Biases and blind spots change with time and shifting cultural mores. Drivers swerving away from one ditch may overcorrect into the other. The goal of a reformation is not to eliminate the need for all future ones. No reformation solves all problems or solves them forever.

In some generations the shifts required may look small. To other generations may fall a more difficult work, responding to a landscape radically reshaped—by Spirit, culture, human error, or all of the above. These are the epoch-marking periods we might in retrospect label as reformations. But what matters most isn't what we call it. What matters is the response, the work of continual recalibration and reorientation that marks faithfulness in any age.

TWENTY-FIRST-CENTURY DISRUPTIONS

Of course, we'd all still like to know—are we now living through a new reformation, a time of particularly widespread and consolidated recalibration in the church? It would be hubris to claim to know for certain. Only history can judge how its chapters will be meaningfully divided. However, we might acknowledge an accumulation of pressures—a widening of fissures—that look strikingly similar to conditions five hundred years ago, when the last Christian reformation erupted.

We saw that the sixteenth-century reformation was set off in no small part by groundbreaking technological developments that altered the information which people had access to and the ways they communicated. The twentieth-century invention of the internet has produced the greatest shifts in knowledge and communication since the printing press. If three people have spiritual revelations after chugging energy drinks and hanging upside-down for half an hour, they can find each other and start a new religion. Ordinary individuals have access to the entire accumulation of human knowledge and exposure to an array of ideas and opinions no previous generation could have imagined existed.

Like the sixteenth-century church, the twenty-first-century church has also been rocked by scandals and abuses. Each week brings new revelations of religious leaders misusing power for sexual gratification or personal financial benefit, an uncovering of cancer in the bones of the church. In many countries, Christian support of nationalistic or racist ideologies raises the question of whom the Christian movement really serves. Indeed, this mistrust of leadership and of institutions is not limited to religion but is rapidly growing across all sectors of society. All institutions, it seems, are vulnerable to co-option and corruption.

Questions of authority, which have been building up since the Enlightenment, also seem to be reaching a cultural tipping point. Science has given way to increasing scientism, a belief in only one way of knowing, making a claim of divine revelation feel equivalent to the claim of a coffee date with the tooth fairy. Materialism reduces the world to physical components and mechanical processes. A swirling storm of contradictory "facts" leaves many wondering who should be believed or if anything can truly be known.

"Scripture alone!"—the rallying cry of authority during the last reformation—has proved much more complicated than its first advocates supposed. Even those who embrace the Bible in theory hotly contest how it applies to life. Meanwhile, rapid shifts in values present powerful challenges to established cultural and religious narratives. Certain biblical portraits of God seem repressive, or sexist, or cruel. Some question whether such an ancient faith could have anything at all to say to the most urgent modern questions.

The result of all these coinciding pressures is a palpable sense of tension and confusion across Christianity. We have heard that ominous, ear-splitting "crack"—even if we don't yet know what it means. It's almost impossible to miss the rumbling beneath our feet. Something, we can't help but suspect, is about to go down.

The buzzword in the air is *deconstruction*; these are the syllable-sounds of the cracking in our time. Many feel alienated from the churches of their upbringing. Some are disavowing Christianity entirely. Many more are adrift in a sea of ambiguity. The possibility of God is hard to rule out. There is something kind of interesting about Jesus. But many are unsure where to go or what any of this means for their relationship to church or Christianity.

Surveys indicate that many of those not leaving the church entirely are switching churches or attending multiple churches at once. Pastors confess struggling to explain to their congregants significant changes in their own faith. Local churches close their doors or gather in diminishing numbers, more unified by politics than any spirituality. Denominations split or rapidly disintegrate as more and more people begin to suspect that nothing but a shared fondness for casserole holds them together any longer.

Of course, religious deconstruction is only one form. Christianity is hardly alone in experiencing upheaval. The same forces of globalization and technological change affecting Christianity are provoking social deconstruction on a massive scale. Notions of leadership and power, gender and family, free speech and free will face powerful questions. What does it mean to be human in a world full of chatbots? What does it mean to be accountable in a society that recognizes the long-term brain effects of trauma? For that matter, what does it mean to make a choice at all if physics points to Many Worlds? For better or worse, deconstruction is the order of the age. This is the larger context of the church's current struggle—an apparent epoch-shift in the existence of humanity itself.

So, then, are we living through a new reformation period? Only time will tell. But there are many reasons to believe that the church has reached another liminal moment. Some will suggest that Christianity has reached its expiration date and is slowly dying out. But others may glimpse within the turmoil the intentional movement of a Spirit who has always excelled at creating out of chaos. They may see in this unraveling an opportunity for overdue change, for repenting, for reorienting, for rediscovering the true shape of the world. This generation, living through one of history's regular hinge points, may yet have a chance to re-form, to renovate the Christian house so that generations to come can flourish faithfully within it. We likely would not have chosen to live in the moment of cliffs crashing. But perhaps God and the moment have chosen us.

SIGNS OF CONVERGENCE

One important sign that God may be up to something is what you might call *convergence*—common themes emerging from diverse quarters simultaneously. This mysterious force was one way the early church rediscovered God's original intent to call all ethnic groups into covenant. Cornelius, a Roman soldier, and Peter, a Jewish fisherman, saw converging visions that drew them toward each other and outside their own established tracks. Paul, a boundary-pushing missionary, and James, a hometown traditionalist, both recognized within their own distinct frames a common truth emerging.

In a tumultuous moment when so many certainties and alliances are coming unmoored, one of the most interesting things a closer observer might notice are potentially discernable track marks of unexpected convergence. Questions asked by people across diverse Christian groups and traditions have striking overlap, as do many first inklings of insight. Leaders across different denominations, countries, and even continents, following their own set of breadcrumbs, are often surprised to look up and find their path intersecting with others they never expected to be near. One reason for this might be because we are not inventing reality but discovering it, all of us being drawn from our starting points by the powerful force of divine gravity.

Convergence is often very slow. It is messy and uneven as we start at different points and move at different speeds and angles. Never has there been a time when everyone reached consensus, nor is this even our primary goal. But much like the process of detecting the location of a star or black hole, evidence may accumulate from diverse objects orbiting a common space, influenced in their motion by a previously unnoticed force acting on them. Whether they are drawn to it or thrown off by it, this is the force, the Reality, with which all must contend.

THE PURPOSE OF THIS BOOK

So where exactly does this book fit within a global conversation about what the Spirit may be up to at this time in history? It is certainly not—and this is important—intended to be *predictive* of the future. I am not drawing on quantitative research to demonstrate exactly which direction the religious winds are blowing. Because God engages the world in partnership with people, different outcomes are always possible depending on how we choose to respond to what the Spirit is stirring. Nor am I pretending to be somehow *objective* about what the outcomes might be. I, like pretty much everyone else, have my own deeply held convictions about what outcomes might be better or worse.

This book is also not a *proposal* for the future of Christianity. For one, nothing I say will be original enough to merit the term. Good theology is often an exercise in theme and variation, taking what we've heard before and inviting us to hear anew. Neither am I bold enough to suppose it is my job to "propose" on behalf of the whole Christian church what it ought to be. The ideas I articulate here come from observation of themes emerging from many living communities who find their faith shifting and growing in common directions.[1]

This book is primarily two things.

---

1. For those interested, I write and teach out of a particular wing of the Christian tradition called Anabaptism, which emerged five hundred years ago during the last reformation. The theological ideas that undergird this book are largely anchored in that stream and will (hopefully) be recognizable to many who inhabit it. However, I have also been vastly enriched by relationship and study with other branches of the Christian family. It's my belief that the emerging movement of the Spirit is far bigger than any one particular branch and will likely challenge and rearrange former ecclesial categories, including my own.

First, it is an expression of hope. I believe there is a more beautiful, faithful, truthful Christian story available than many versions that have taken hold in recent centuries. And I believe there is a chance we are living in a time when that better story may be widely rediscovered. The favored words used to tell the story may vary by clan and culture. There will almost certainly remain edges and subplots on which we'll disagree. But there is an essential narrative arc, a common, golden core pulsing with power that I believe is truly there to be uncovered. And I have hope that something could emerge in this moment of Great Cracking that looks more like Jesus and the revolution he began. This book is therefore written from my prayers and hopes for the church that could be.

There are plenty of indications that this greater movement is already taking shape, as people around the world are being stirred by the Spirit toward a set of common rediscoveries. I am only one among many who are finding ourselves awakening to a bigger story than we once imagined. The movement is owned not by any person, group, or institution but by the One who is gently summoning all of us from many directions at once.

Second, this book is written as an invitation to a communal conversation. The question of what the future of Christianity should be extends far beyond any one individual, church, organization, or tradition. It's a question of what Jesus' story is really about, where we've drifted from it, where church and culture are hitting dead ends, and what sort of hope God's presence offers. If we are to have any prayer of answering these questions well, we desperately need each other in order to see what is in our blind spots. Diverse wings of the church may be carrying critical pieces of the answers we are seeking, and only when they are put together will the whole picture emerge.

Therefore I come to this conversation not with arrogant certainty but with both passionate conviction and awareness of the limits of my vision, hoping to invite a dialogue. If this renewal is truly from God, it will be guided and midwifed by the Spirit in many places at once as communities across the globe enter into deep, humble, hope-filled conversation with each other across long-standing divides.

The hopes expressed in this book are not mine alone but are actively emerging from the early stages of a dialogue. They are longings shared by a growing community of hopefuls around the world. The genesis of the book itself came in conversation with a group of pastors, theologians, and curious Christians who had connected with each other through a network of churches and leaders called Jesus Collective. We had come from many countries and Christian traditions, drawn together by a common restlessness. "What are we really searching for?" we asked ourselves and each other. The answer that emerged from our own small dialogue felt both simple and radical: we are seeking a Christianity that thinks and acts more like Jesus.

So many people I've spoken to in recent years across diverse contexts express a yearning to hear someone say in the open what they are seeing and sensing. To acknowledge the pain points and itches. To name where the church has been telling a story they no longer buy because it looks nothing like the One who founded it. Many of us long to discover we aren't alone in feeling this way. More than that, we long for conversation partners who are ready to dream and labor with us toward the emergence of a better story.

If you are looking for theological innovation, this book is probably not for you. I have little of it to offer here, and in fact I suspect that innovation sometimes functions as a Western cultural idol born of our endless appetite for novelty and our tendency to confuse what is newest with what is truest.

If you come to this conversation as someone currently deconstructing your previous faith, fair play to you. When you hit a dead end, the only sensible thing to do is to turn around and rethink your previous route. There are things we all must unthink, must unlearn to find the path forward again. But the coming apart is only stage one. The Spirit is working in the church to help us collectively put the pieces back together in a way that is somehow both ancient and new.

If you come to this conversation not so much because you are deconstructing but because you believe to your bones there is *more* for the church and for the world in Jesus than we are yet embracing, then I can only say I'm delighted for your companionship in discerning the next move of God. The last reformation centered on a recovery of Scripture. The next reformation may well involve a recentering on Jesus Christ and a fresh encounter with the Spirit he loosed.

THE STRUCTURE OF THIS BOOK

In the chapters ahead, I describe eight rediscoveries that I hope and believe could mark a much-needed renewal for the next age of Christianity. I begin each chapter by describing a significant pain point that many have encountered in the Christian story to which they've been exposed. In each "Dilemma" section, I attempt to name as honestly as possible the real questions many of us are holding and the holes we see in answers we have been given by the church. I also suggest how secular Western culture—culture emerging as Christianity recedes and pluralism and skepticism become dominant forces—is offering its own responses to similar questions and hitting its own dead ends.

From there, we will make a turn toward Jesus, considering where a response to our dilemmas that centers on him might begin. In the "Rediscovery" sections we'll search for a hinge point, a critical insight or shift in understanding within the Jesus story that might open an alternative way of being. And finally, in the sections titled "Transformation," we'll explore what a life, a church, a world shaped by this fresh vision could look like. We'll consider what it could mean to truly inhabit the rediscovery.

Readers will note that I have chosen to structure this conversation about reformation with a series of theological propositions—"rediscoveries"—in a manner reminiscent of Luther's theses (though with far fewer than ninety-five— you're welcome). I am keenly aware of the weaknesses of this approach. One might argue that one of the problems with the Western church is its tendency to too highly value abstract propositions over mystery and embodied faith. I take this critique seriously. There are many conversations that can and must be had about where and why our theory has been disconnected from our practice, about the limits of human speech and category, about the critical role of mystical encounter and the many kinds of knowing.

These conversations are no less crucial than the one we are about to have. So why not start the new reformation dialogue with an exploration of practice instead of theology? In large part because I believe that human beings are fundamentally storytellers. Stories are the way we make meaning, order our lives, understand ourselves, others, and God. They are containers within which we live, setting the boundaries of our vision, the possibilities and limits of our practice. A beautiful story does not inevitably result in beautiful living. But the beauty of our living will rarely outrun the beauty of the story we hold.

Theology, I believe, is a version of storytelling. It is the art of telling a story about God and us and the world that aligns with the greatest truth, goodness, and beauty we know. This is why Christian theology begins and ends with Jesus. He is the story that God has chosen to tell—about God and about humanity.

At the end of the day, the critical work of integrating story into embodied practice is deeply contextual. Churches, communities, and collectives gathered around Jesus all over the world will find ways of living into and out of his story that reflect the uniqueness of their particular settings and circumstances. This work of local contextualization is a crucial part of the invitation—and opportunity—that lies ahead of all of us.

Therefore, having considered the difference it makes to recenter our story on Jesus, I will pass the baton onto you. This conversation is ultimately one for you, the reader, to open with the Jesus followers and Jesus-curious people in your life. What problems do you see in the church's status quo or in the story the church has been telling? What would a more faithful, hopeful, Jesus-centered Christianity look like? Why do you think so? How would it be practiced on the ground, in your own local context?

For better or worse—often both—God chooses to work relationally, inviting us into partnership with the Spirit in the emergence of what will be. It is wonderful, dangerous work we are embarking on together. How better to begin, then, than with a prayer of surrender, hunger, and grace. We pray as Jesus followers have through every age and through every change:

God who loves us, first and forever,
    may all creation recognize—and echo—your goodness.

Make earth like heaven, exactly how you want it,
   a manifestation of your dreams.
Give us what we need to flourish and serve today.
Forgive us for the things we inevitably get wrong,
   as we show grace to others who are also screwing up.
Please stretch us, but not to the point our faith breaks.
Deliver us from all that deceives and distorts,
   within us and around us.
Let this be so.
Amen.

CONVERSATION STARTERS

1. Do you believe we may be on the cusp of another reformation period? Why or why not?
2. What do you think might lie at the center of a new reformation, if indeed one is emerging?
3. Where do you think the church is in greatest need of reform?
4. What do you hope for when you think of what the next age of the church could look like?
5. What concerns or cautions do you have about the idea of embracing a "reformation rethink" of Christian faith?

1

The Great Yardstick

A Changed Approach to Scripture

DILEMMA

THE MANY GODS PROBLEM

In a pluralistic age when core beliefs range from atheism to aliens-built-the-pyramids, one might assume that the people whom Christians feel closest to are other Jesus-y types. I mean, the cross has the same shape whether it's embroidered on pillows or tattooed on biceps, am I right?

Ha.

Of course, this is patently *not* the present situation. If religious people are often a mystery to our nonreligious neighbors, we're no less mystifying to each other. Many Christians today find themselves staring slack-jawed at other Christians from the opposite side of the information highway, wondering, "What on earth is wrong with you guys?"

Headlines might trumpet the decline of Christianity, but there are still quite a few of us around—a few billion professing Christians, give or take. These Christians are divided into roughly forty-five thousand distinct Christian denominations, each one championing its own set of claims—claims about who God is, about what God wants, about what (or whom) God hates.

It's not like these claims differ only in small ways on the margins, like brands of ranch dressing. The claims are frequently flat contradictions of each other. Listen to different Christian groups speaking of God, and it sounds like one is extolling peanut butter while the other exegetes socks; it's hard at times to tell whether they're even in the same conversation.

The stakes of the stories we tell about God are extraordinarily high. This much is evident even (sometimes especially) to those who don't believe in God. Every person—religious believer or religious skeptic—must live by some story of what is real or what is good, and every story has practical consequences.

If your fundamental belief is that the world is composed of a scarce amount of goods and that only the fittest survive, odds are good this story influences both your politics and what you'll personally do to climb the ladder. If you believe there is a God who loves you deeply and despises your opponents, chances are your workplace and holiday table all show the effects. If you're truly convinced that there is a God who is reliably generous, or a God who raises the dead, it alters the calculations of what can be shared or risked. If you believe there is a God who loves justice but performs no miracles and has no hands but those that humans lend, this too affects the calculus of possibility.

Conservative. Progressive. Religious. Atheist. There's no way to not have a story. There's no way to avoid its impact.

Here we are running around the world, billions of so-called Christians, belonging to tens of thousands of groups, each telling a story about God and God's desires. And the results are truly astonishing in their breadth and diversity. Hospitals and universities founded. Also book burnings and inquisitions. Amish buggies and papal palaces. In Russia, God blessing an invasion while in Ukraine, God is summoned against it. In Rwanda, God apparently endorsing genocide but also enabling unthinkable forgiveness. In the United States, believers lobbing memes in God's defense from opposite sides of every cultural picket line.

How is a person supposed to tell which vision of God is right? I mean, we haven't met, but I assume you are one of those with the right ideas. But how do you know, and why should anyone else believe this? What's at stake here is not just a matter of personal, inward belief. It may start or stop wars, make or break families, tip elections or influence the outcome of plagues. This is no hyperbole. God-stories have done all these things, in less time than those someday-I'll-fit-them jeans have been sitting in the back of your closet.

THE BIG BOOK PROBLEM

What makes this whole situation even more confusing is, if you ask diverse Christians where they got their ideas about God and what God wants, most will give the same answer: "The Bible!" The majority acknowledge this one book as their starting point, or at least as a key touchstone, in negotiating truth.

Indeed, it was the last reformation that brought the unique role of the Bible into focus. The sixteenth-century reformers discovered the power of the Bible as a crucial counterweight to the power of institutions and leaders. This book possessed an authority that could call human corruption to account.

Scripture also provided a kind of neutral ground on which theological disputes could be mediated. It was an arbiter of truth that no pope or faction could control.

The assumption of the reformers at the start of the Protestant Reformation was that if the Bible could only be freed from the stranglehold of elites and the deadweight of tradition, everyone would read and see the plain truth for themselves: "Hey guys, groundbreaking idea here—what if we just read the book . . . and do whatever it says?" Nothing could seem more sensible.

It swiftly became apparent, however, that things were not quite so simple. If you give the Bible to diverse people, with different nationalities, experiences, educations, and investments, it turns out that many will hear quite different things. There's a decent chance that most will find some verse or story that seems to confirm their existing inclinations.

The sixteenth century found verses for creating religious art and verses for destroying it. There were verses for fomenting peasant revolt and for supporting the nobles who squashed it. Five centuries later, we are befuddled by the same problem. There are verses for those who support the death penalty and for those who march against it. There are verses for feminists and for those who subscribe to traditional gender roles. There are verses for turning the other cheek and verses to chant while rallying the troops. The "neutral ground" of Scripture is hotly contested territory.

A few—the true nerd-warriors among us—get out of bed for an exegetical throwdown. Talented preachers get rich and famous selling biblical code-breaking tools. But deep down, what many of us worry we've learned from five hundred years and forty-five thousand denominations is that the biblical emperor has no clothes. Maybe everyone is just sort of making it up, like in one of those "choose your own adventure" books where if you don't like where the tale comes out, you can go back and take another fork in the road.

Questions about the book extend to the God the book describes. Taken in plain sense, the God whom one page calls "friend of sinners" seems on another page despotic and maybe genocidal. The very same inspired law code that institutes the radical social equity policy of regular debt cancellation also orders the execution of rebellious sons. It's hard to know who such a God really is, or what this God would or wouldn't do.

When it comes to resolving deep questions of God's character and desires, our preexisting, often highly politicized ideologies tend to prescribe the possible set of solutions in play. If I and my people (whomever they are) wouldn't do it, value it, believe it, choose it, then surely it could not be true. The inward turn of authority across Western culture renders external challenge of any kind particularly difficult. It isn't clear what sort of evidence—biblical or otherwise—should be permitted to override personal intuition or contemporary cultural values.

Because of all these factors, an increasing number of people—including Christians—are quietly setting the Bible aside. They still believe, or want to believe, in a loving God. They are still trying to live by a set of values they were taught— at least some of them, the ones that seem reasonable enough. They may well still go to church and value the community. But the book itself feels too contradictory to untangle and too unsettling to be trusted. Better to just say our prayers, try to be good, and trust our gut to tell us what's true and right.

THE PUZZLE OF PLURALISM

The Bible was once, at the very least, a respected moral document, but in the world outside the church, at least among educated elites, there is a growing feeling that it has outlived its cultural shelf-life and is starting to smell. The Bible, some say, is oppressive, anti-woman, and anti-science. It celebrates a violent God who in turn sanctions human violence. It might contain a record of past moral advances, but we twenty-first-century people have evolved beyond it.

While the Western world may be increasingly over the notion of divine revelation, however, the end of religion has certainly not marked the end of truth claims. It's easy to file the Bible next to *The Odyssey* and other tomes that you skimmed once in college and now keep on the shelf just to impress dates with the breadth of your erudition. We can snap the cords that bind us to an angry God or the oppression of formal religion. It's much harder, however, to shake the intuition that some things are right and others are wrong.

Religious people have hardly cornered the market on moral outrage. Listen to a political podcast of virtually any stripe, and you'll hear language thick with moral conviction and moral disgust. Rarely are these intuitions interrogated or traced to their origins. They are simply experienced and assumed to be shared with the audience. Some things just *feel* so obviously good or viscerally wicked, no defense should be required.

The trouble is, what is obvious to one is not so obvious to all. Bone-deep intuitions frequently conflict. Headlines are full of violent public clashes between groups equally convinced of their cause's righteousness. One culture's definition of liberty—bikini, anyone?—another culture sees as exploitative and demeaning. Seemingly self-evident facts about reality are disputed, and narratives making sense of the world fundamentally diverge. Social media speeds this divergence along, blurring the lines between facts and opinions.

In a connected age, pluralism is raising a profoundly difficult set of questions for people around the world. With so many sources making competing claims about truth, reality, and goodness, which voices should we trust, and why? This is a surprisingly hard question to answer, as many have discovered debating Uncle Bob the moon-landing-denier from across the holiday table. What do we accept as evidence that something is true? How much evidence is enough? What do we do when our deepest intuitions of right and wrong conflict? How exactly are contradictory beliefs about truth or goodness to be arbitrated?

There are many ways to answer these questions without defaulting to religion. None, however, are less complicated. We might say, "Let 'good' stand for whatever supports human flourishing and let us call 'evil' what opposes it." But of course, what constitutes "flourishing" is itself subjective and disputed. Some recommend alignment with "the right side of history," but a recent flurry of alternative history books suggest that history's outcomes may be far more contingent than we think. Anyway, do we really want to say something is right simply because it *wins*?

Swimming in a sea of ambiguity and misinformation and recognizing the high stakes in the stories of reality we tell, many of us would perhaps like to believe in the existence of an ultimate Truth. We would like to think that history has an arc that bends toward justice. But even if such a Truth exists, how would we know what it is? And while we might feel an aching nostalgia for the security of a universal justice-keeper, that doesn't mean we're prepared to accept some "outside force" defining the meaning of justice for us.

REDISCOVERY

THE ORIGIN STORY OF CHRISTIANITY

The global movement we now know as Christianity began for one simple reason: a small group of people in an overlooked corner of the Roman Empire became convinced that an executed criminal had shown them what God is like. Put that way, it sounds bizarre, like the sort of weirdness you'd expect from ancient people who laundered clothes in urine. Except . . . these people were not so different from us at all. Far from confirming their preexisting biases, this conclusion contradicted their deepest beliefs and expectations.

The Jewish people were the world's first monotheists. Generations had fought and died to defend the conviction that God should not be depicted in any concrete form. The Roman emperor's divine pretensions were a source of intellectual and moral disgust. During the first century, the Jewish homeland was occupied by Rome, with tensions running high. The people were searching for a political savior, a military leader, to turn the tables of regional power and restore national sovereignty. Many ambitious men had tried and quickly met their demise.

When Jesus of Nazareth broke onto the public scene as a teacher speaking about God's desires, what struck many listeners first was the ring of authority in his voice. Jesus wasn't the only traveling preacher at this time who claimed to speak for God. But something about him felt different, laden with a mysterious weight and clarity no one had encountered before. Jesus claimed that God was more wildly gracious and generous than anybody had ever imagined. In a world full of religious voices shouting over each other, his cut through the noise without even being raised.

What distinguished Jesus from other teachers wasn't just his talk. It was also the deeds that backed his words up. The Jewish people had witnessed miracles before, outbreaks of divine graciousness and freedom for which there was no known natural explanation. Their history was full of such events. But there was little precedent for something like this—so many unexplainable, powerful happenings clustered around a single person.

Everywhere Jesus went, those who encountered him became more whole, more fully alive. His apprentices even watched nature seemingly respond to his voice. These incidents did not confirm some prior conviction but rather created an increasingly perplexing and unsettling question: Who on earth *was* this guy?

But perhaps even more remarkable than Jesus' words or miracles was his character. Jesus didn't seem interested in leveraging his growing fame to acquire some better job or social position. Precisely the opposite, in fact. He left places when crowds grew too large. He tried to dial down the stories when they began to go viral. At every opportunity, he declined the chance for personal advancement. Instead, he modeled consistently the very qualities he claimed for God—humility, patience, compassion, generosity.

Character is easy to overlook, especially from a distance. But in an era when we've witnessed leader after leader fall to private weakness, it's worth pausing to marvel a bit. The first thing Jesus did in his public ministry was invite twelve people—with quite diverse worldviews—to follow him around, to hear everything he said and see everything he did. They traveled with him and slept beside him on the ground every night. They were with him nearly every minute for years. They saw him tired, hungry, grieving, in conflict, and in pain.

What they witnessed was courage that never broke, integrity that never faltered, insight that was never mistaken, compassion that never went cold. Even false witnesses paid to testify against him couldn't find a convincing story.

But regardless of Jesus' innocence, his opponents succeeded in getting him executed. That's where the story seems destined to end—with the marvelous and mystifying Jesus of Nazareth inaugurated into an elite pantheon of prophets and martyrs like Isaiah and Martin Luther King Jr. Except there is one more twist to his story. Hundreds of people who knew Jesus intimately, who'd watched his execution, who'd wrapped his dead body and sealed it in a tomb, encountered him again. And they didn't just see or hear him, like some ghostly apparition—they ate fish he cooked for them with his own hands; they touched the torn flesh of his sword-hole.

Then, and only then, did the unlikely answer begin to dawn on Jesus' friends and family to their question, "Who is this?" Only then did his outrageous claims—"Whoever has seen me has seen the Father" (John 14:9)—begin to register in their full meaning. Jesus spoke like a prophet and died like a martyr. But unlike the rest, God had brought Jesus back. What greater endorsement could they ask for? What louder way could God declare, "Listen to this guy! He's been speaking for and embodying me!" They would give the remainder of their lives—and in almost all cases, embrace grisly deaths—to let others know what they'd heard.

Even Jesus' biological brother ultimately became one of his followers and a devoted leader in the early Jesus movement. Known as James the Righteous, Jesus' brother was famed not just among Christians but among the wider Jewish community for his integrity. This very James, who played with Jesus in the sandbox, lived with him through his hormone-rushing teens, was there when he hit his thumb with the hammer learning carpentry, threw in his lot with the community of people who concluded they'd experienced something in Jesus so singular that nothing but the direct invention of God in the world could account for it.

THE MEANING OF JESUS

The statements that the early church made about Jesus are extraordinary in both their scope and their conclusions. One of Jesus' closest companions for years, a fisherman named John, writes about him, "Grace and truth came into being through Jesus Christ. No one has ever seen God. God the only Son, who is at the Father's side, has made God known" (John 1:17–18). Paul, a brilliant Jewish scholar who was one of early Christianity's fiercest opponents, encountered Jesus in such a convincing way—after Jesus' death—that Paul would write of him, "The Son is the image of the invisible God. . . . All the fullness of God was pleased to live in him" (Colossians 1:15, 19). The anonymous author of Hebrews, a devoted student of Israel's history, declares, "In the past, God spoke through the prophets to our ancestors in many times and many ways. In these final days, though, he spoke to us through a Son. . . . The Son is the light of God's glory and the imprint of God's being" (Hebrews 1:1–3). These conclusions, from such fierce mono-theists, were likely only conceivable because of what they'd heard from Jesus himself: "I am in the Father and the Father is in me" (John 14:11).

These people who knew Jesus best, who either were first-hand witnesses to his life or knew those witnesses personally, became convinced that what had occurred in Jesus was entirely without precedent. There had been many true prophets, many true visions and dreams. There had been fire from heaven, ten commandments, many midnight whispers from God. But here, in this Galilean, was something more. The Playwright who had always been working behind the scenes of history had chosen for a moment to step onto the stage to speak the lines no one else could be trusted to deliver, play the role no other actor could properly perform.

The early Christians were very clear: Jesus was not God's "softer side." All the fullness of an infinite God that could fit within a mortal body was contained in Jesus. Jesus was God's authorized representative, sent to set straight the record about who God is, about what God wants, about how reality really operates. He revealed these truths with his words and with the entirety of his life. Jesus was the one true and accurate divine image bearer. He was a revelation of the truth about God and a revelation of the truth about what humanity, made in God's image, is meant to become.

Yes, these are extraordinary claims. The early Christians were very much aware of that fact. They came to believe them under the extraordinary evidence of the resurrection. We of course must decide for ourselves whether we find their testimony credible. Whatever our difficulty imagining that God would enter the world in this way, this at least should cause us to wonder: Who among us could hold up to such scrutiny that our friends and family would conclude of us, "This one is grace and truth embodied"?

JESUS AND THE WORD OF GOD

Having experienced Jesus in this way and drawn such conclusions about him, the early Jesus followers were left in a complex relationship with other words, insights, and revelations ascribed to God. Significantly, the early church did not conclude that no other truths about God or the world or right and wrong had been revealed apart from Jesus. They did not believe that Jesus was the only one through whom God had ever spoken. Indeed, they could not believe these things while listening to Jesus. Jesus himself taught the Hebrew Scriptures as authoritative, a reliable representation of a love story between God and the people of Israel that had been unfolding for centuries. He had come as the culmination of this love story, not a separate tale. Many of his teachings were deeply rooted in the genuine insights of prophetic encounters from the past. Jesus revealed a God who had been communicating and acting throughout history, both within Israel and outside it.

Furthermore, one of the most astonishing claims of the first Jesus followers was that there would be a time after Jesus when many, many more prophets would enter the scene. Hours before his death, Jesus had told his followers that he had more still to say that they weren't ready for yet. But that was okay, he assured them, because neither death nor departure could shut him up. Communication would continue. In the new era of history that he was about to set in motion, there would be an explosion in the number of people equipped to hear from God for themselves. The early church quickly discovered that this God-hearing power wasn't to be limited to first-century Jewish people. It included enemy soldiers, foreigners, women, children—people they never imagined. God was getting more vocal in this new chapter, not less.

So then, the early Christians knew that the word of the Lord had come before and would come again many times and in many ways. At the same time, having met Jesus, they had made a game-changing discovery: not all words or truths are equal. There is a qualitative difference between hearing God's words from another person, even a good and wise one, and hearing them from God's own mouth.

Moses, Israel's greatest hero, went up Mount Sinai to receive the law on Israel's behalf because the rest of the people were too afraid to hear God's voice (Exodus 20:19). One man became a mediator of God's words for the rest. But in Jesus, God had come down from the mountain. Jesus was greater than Moses, the early Jesus followers controversially concluded, because while Moses was perhaps history's most remarkable messenger, Jesus was the message. He wasn't just delivering it—he *was* it. God's compassion, embodied. God's Word fleshed, incarnated, made visible, a picture more evocative than an infinity of words.

As Jesus' friend John puts it, Jesus was the Word with God in the beginning, before a single other word was written or heard (John 1:1). Jesus is what God has always been speaking, trying to get humanity to understand. Jesus is the revelation of the true meaning behind every line. Every time God speaks or has ever spoken, the sound of that voice has been Jesus.

A NEW LENS ON SCRIPTURE

This conviction about the unique clarity of God's revelation in Jesus led the early Christians to take a new approach in their relationship to scripture—at that time, made up of the texts we now call the Old Testament. They accepted these books, as Jesus did, as a truthful witness to God's engagement with humanity and as an authoritative guide to a faithful life. They did not, however, accept them as authoritative when read just any way. Scripture that the early Christians accepted as authoritative was scripture interpreted *in light of Jesus*, who had definitively revealed God's heart and clarified God's intent. Not every way of construing the words of the Bible was equally accurate and good. Every word attributed to God, whether past or future, must now be measured against the culminating revelation of Jesus himself.

According to Luke, who meticulously researched and documented Jesus' ministry, on the very day of his resurrection, Jesus sought out a few of his old followers and began teaching them how to read scripture backward from him (Luke 24:27). A large portion of the collection of letters and stories now known as the Christian New Testament are exercises in re-reading. Their authors went back to the stories of Adam and Eve, Sarah and Abraham, Pharaoh and Moses, the temple, kingship and prophets, and asked what emerged from these stories as now viewed in Jesus' clarifying light.

What they saw sometimes surprised them: layers of nuance, of meaning and intent, that weren't always evident before. It turned out that faith, a deep personal trust, had always been God's core desire. It turned out that the Canaanite idolaters and Egyptian captors who had seemed the story's villains were themselves also captives whom God longed to save. It turned out that the temple and sacrifices were signposts but not the final destination.

Scripture repeatedly commanded, "Be holy like God is." Many had understood holiness to be a measure of distance from badness. But Jesus modeled holiness in fearless proximity, as a purifying force that drew the healing power of grace and truth toward the infected and deceived.

Scripture said, "Love your neighbor." Most had intuited that a neighbor must be a God-fearing person who looks and thinks like you. Neighbors certainly weren't people who threatened you or foreigners who worshiped other gods. But when Jesus is asked how God defines *neighbor*, he describes an anonymous stranger lying beside the road who could be literally anyone—including the guy who rides around with that appalling bumper sticker stuck to the back of his donkey (Luke 10:25–37). Jesus even explicitly counts in the category of neighbor the enemy seeking your harm (Matthew 5:43–48).

Many teachers before Jesus had suggested that love was the fulfillment of God's law. On this Jesus firmly agreed. But he also insisted on defining *which* love meets the conditions. The love that God was seeking wasn't easy affection for those who return it or a thing that can be discarded when the cost gets high. Love that fulfills God's law is indiscriminate, impractically patient, inconveniently faithful. It is love that gives without calculation, without keeping records, without expectation of a return invitation or even a thank-you note (Luke 6:27–36).

God's Word had been there all along, but it turned out that no one's intuitions had been up to the challenge of truly grasping the radicality of God's moral imagination. What had been needed was not just the words themselves but the interpretative key to unlocking them. Jesus himself was the interpretative key, throwing open every God-intended meaning.

COMPLETING THE LAST REFORMATION

So here we are in the twenty-first century, swimming in competing claims about God, truth, and reality. Collectively haunted by the discovery that there is no self-evident "fact of things." All ground is disputed. Every word has multiple meanings. The puzzle pieces frustratingly fit together in more than one possible way. We cannot unknow these things, no matter how deep our longing for simpler times with greater supposed certainties.

Nor does the traditional Christian answer since the sixteenth-century reformation—"Just believe the inspired

Book!"—suffice. Because there are many ways to understand what the book is saying. And there are many questions we feel pressed to ask that the book does not address. A first-century subject index meets a twenty-first-century context with uneasy gaps.

We can acknowledge the realities frankly and openly because, contrary to what many have feared, they do not spell the end either of truth or of Christianity. Instead, they constitute an invitation to rediscover what always lay at the Christian foundation: truth embodied in a person—God's Word, living and incarnate.

REDISCOVERY #1:

Jesus is the authoritative lens through which God is seen and the Bible is interpreted.

In many ways, this rediscovery lies at the end of a long road the church began walking down five centuries ago. Facing a crisis of confused and corrupted authority, the Protestant Reformers cried, "Scripture alone!" This was a critical corrective in their day and a crucial starting point, but the conclusion was not yet complete. It stopped short of the revolutionary insight that first birthed Christianity: truth, love, justice, has a face. The one who has seen Jesus has seen what is good and real. By Jesus all truth claims are measured. A reformation that centers on Scripture perhaps inevitably leads to a reformation that centers on Jesus, through whom Scripture is understood.

TRANSFORMATION

A NEW YARDSTICK

Christianity from its very beginning was centered on Jesus. He is the foundation on which all authority is built. But we lost track of this fact for a while. Much of the church has gotten caught up in other stories about God and truth. The result is our present situation, where many Christians are toppling alongside their neighbors into a chasm of nihilism and fast-fashion ideologies. Intuitions collide with no way to mediate them—a clash of gods with no arbiter.

Jesus is the arbiter. That is the core insight at the heart of Christianity. You can take it or leave it, believe it or doubt it, but this is the central claim on which Christianity rises and falls: God looks, has always looked, will always look, like Jesus. Jesus is the revelation of both creation's design and where history's arc will land. He is the field, the stable frame within which our deepest questions about reality are asked.

Practically speaking, what this means is that the truth now has a yardstick. There are many sources of potentially true information about the world. Scripture, as we have seen. Science, a method for seeking truth written in the material stuff of creation. Beauty. Reason. Intuition. Mystical experience. Experience of the more everyday variety. All of these are potential sources of knowledge. None should be disdained. God delights in being sought with every sense and faculty and gives some piece of God's self to every form of human knowing.

All these sources can lead us toward genuine truth. But all can also mislead. Or perhaps it is better to say that we can mislead ourselves through them.

Recent years have seen the retraction of hundreds of well-established scientific studies as we have learned more of the ways that human bias creeps into experiments. Psychologists tell us that some of the most dangerous human beings among us—psychopaths—are often good at feigning beauty (for a while).[1] The pursuit of "reason," which turns out to be vulnerable to all manner of cultural and personal biases, has led some to practice eugenics and many others to assume divine sanction for war. Intuition, at least for some, made slavery seem "natural." Mystical experience has prompted murder as well as compassion and sacrifice. The emotional residue of life experience can illuminate but also blind.

God has always understood this dilemma, recognized the deep vulnerability of our embodied knowing. Jesus is God's response. The Christian practice of discernment involves carrying each idea, word, and insight into the presence of Jesus to test for alignment. We hold it up to his words, his work, his life, his death and resurrection. And we ask how it looks when measured against his definitive embodiment of God's character and desires. Writing to his community, the early Christian writer John states the principle simply: "Every spirit that doesn't confess Jesus is not from God" (1 John 4:3). John makes clear that the confession to which he refers is not a mere verbal claim but a *bodied conformity*. If the output of our insight-seeking is incompatible with Jesus, somewhere there's a bug in the code.

WHICH JESUS?

The skeptics among us will be the first to observe that this Jesus-centric approach to truth doesn't magically solve all our problems. The answer to our questions might be "Jesus," but which Jesus exactly are we talking about? Jesus the table-tossing prizefighter? Or Jesus the long-lashed sheep-snuggler? Jesus the conservative values defender? Or Jesus the progressive rabble-rouser? Doesn't this entire line of argument just relocate the dilemma so now we fight over Jesus instead of God in general?

Yes and no. Anyone looking for truth that somehow rises above the "taint" of human subjectivity will not find it in Christianity. This is the story of a God who chose to self-express supremely as a person, not a proposition. A God who chose to write the divine autobiography on human hearts instead of paper. There's no way around the glorious mess of relational knowledge.

But this is also not a person we are inventing from thin air. Jesus' recorded words, preserved by reliable witnesses, cut off some trajectories and opened others. For example, the entire New Testament—including the Gospels and Letters—highlights Jesus' crucifixion and resurrection as the centerpiece of his story. Recognizing as the early church clearly did that Jesus' self-sacrificial death lies at the heart of his movement and revelation of God puts essential definition to God's character and methods of engaging with the world. The cross serves as Jesus' definitive response to portraits of a violent God. Any God embodied by Jesus must be understood within a cross-shaped frame of willing, self-sacrificial, enemy-saving love.[2]

Jesus' actions, his lived (and dying) choices, offer an interpretative context in which his teachings must be heard. There are multiple ways to understand many scenes, but not an infinity of them. Early Christians called themselves "followers of the Way." Not every step of this Way might be mapped out

---

2. For a deeper exploration of this theme, I recommend Greg Boyd's book *Cross Vision: How the Crucifixion of Jesus Makes Sense of Old Testament Violence* (Minneapolis: Fortress Press, 2017).

unambiguously, but more than enough is clear to indicate the direction of true north.

Furthermore, in speaking of Jesus, we are not all just speculating on a historically distant abstraction. If the Christian story holds any water at all, we are speaking of someone who is present and living. Jesus can still speak and act for himself. He is not utterly helpless in the face of human manipulation. He still makes his presence known. He's been known to disrupt narratives that too long misrepresent him. He still owns his story and takes a hand in shaping it.[3]

LIVING THE BOOK

This conversation about "which Jesus" inevitably brings us back to the Bible as a key source of our knowledge of him. Lord have mercy on the modern arrogance of believing that all truth starts and ends with us, that we alone in all of history see clearly and without bias. We've embraced ultra-low-rise jeans, friends. We can get things profoundly wrong! We are one generation among many who have listened carefully for truth, for God. We have much to learn from the insights and experience of those who have walked this way before us.

More than that, as we have seen, Christians follow a person who lived *in history*, who had real eyewitnesses. The Christian New Testament is a carefully researched and tested compilation of their testimonies. Scripture anchors the story of God outside the inscrutability of our private minds,

---

3. This shaping may take a variety of forms. I've met people whose course has been altered by the insight of a prophetic person who saw what was hidden and called out deep distortions in their thinking and living. I know of others who have been corrected by the appearance of Jesus in a vision or dream, or by the quiet whisper of the Spirit that stopped them in their tracks and challenged their assumptions. Sometimes Jesus' intervention may look like a radical disruption in the status quo of a system or institution that forces a reckoning and a significant rethink.

in events of history. It provides a check against the biases of individuals and the biases of our particular age. It is an introduction to Jesus by those who knew him first and who experienced his power to shatter their own biases and upend their own worlds.

When we come to this book, there is a particular method to reading that is distinctively Christian. We read this book looking for Jesus, and we read it through the lens of Jesus. This dual pattern of reading frees the book to serve its role of challenging and transforming our image of God. We read the Old Testament stories with Jesus in mind. We ask how he illuminates and changes meaning, how he exposes blind spots and upends assumptions, how he challenges portraits, how he completes ancient stories or expands on their wisdom. We read the New Testament stories with Jesus in mind. We ask what the first witnesses heard from him most clearly, what his life and death tell us about how God works. We also ask what we can learn about the process of discernment from the first Christian communities who brought Jesus home to new contexts and questions he didn't directly address.

As the story of Jesus spread across the world, his followers sought to contextualize his revelation in new communities and cultures—a practice documented particularly in the New Testament letters. They listened for God's ongoing speech in response to new circumstances. They recognized that the need for interchange between divine words and the divine Word (that is, Jesus) was never going to end. Because there would always be new questions. And because God was never going to cease engaging and interacting. They viewed this prospect not with fear but with high confidence. Each potential word and insight could be measured against what Jesus had revealed about God's character and mission. The Letters in this sense are not just a record of the church's conclusions but a *model* for Jesus-anchored thinking and discernment in every age.[4]

The book is not the end point of the Christian story but a springboard into a God-thick world that is still emerging. This is a story that is still being written. In our world. In our communities. In us. As we live our part, we have a definitive standard of measurement for every claim that can be made of God and God's desires. Whatever unexpected twists or turns the plot takes, whatever questions may arise, God will never speak a word that contradicts Jesus. Because Jesus was there when the story began, the true architect of its design. And he will be there when it ends, the shape of its forever. God looks like Jesus. Always.

TESTING TRUTH

Here's good news for those who have cringed away from ugly stories of ugly gods: the Jesus to which the first witnesses attest does not support oppression or abuse. He isn't anti-science or anti-body. He never condones violence or hate. Jesus radically expands the definition of neighbor. He calls for a life devoted to others' flourishing. He proclaims the end of fear. Jesus says God is an indiscriminate lover—even of the haters. God answers curse with blessing and forgives without counting. If this Jesus and his vision of Reality compels you, then God is for you. Don't let any bad Christian God-talk convince you otherwise.

At the end of the day, either Jesus knows what he's talking about or he doesn't. Some might say that from here you must "take it on faith." But that's not how Jesus spoke about these

---

4. My previous book, *The Bible Unwrapped: Making Sense of Scripture Today* (Harrisonburg, VA: Herald Press, 2018), offers a more in-depth introduction to what it looks like to read all sections of the Bible through the lens of Jesus.

things. Instead, Jesus said to people around him, "Follow me, and see." Follow him around for a while, take the stakes seriously, and see what comes of it. Trust is involved, of course. But not blind trust. If Jesus is what he claims, there should be a measure of conformity between what he says and the shape of emergent reality.

We all must live by some story. The practical question for most of us is simply whether Jesus' story is worth a try, whether the vision Jesus casts of a world . . .

> where God cares even for the birds
> and pays close enough attention
> to know your post-shower hair count,
> where the poor get fed
> and those drowning in excess
> get the gift of empty,
> where people pay their enemies' bills
> and stumbling is forgiven
> as we all learn to walk upright

is beautiful enough to be worth testing for its truth.

CONVERSATION STARTERS

1. Why do you think people have such different pictures of God and God's character? Where do these ideas come from?

2. What does it mean to read the Bible through the lens of Jesus? How might this look different from any other approach?

3. What do we learn about God, truth, or reality through Jesus that we wouldn't have known otherwise?

4. What do you think would change practically in the church if we rediscovered the core truth that God looks like Jesus?

5. Where do you think the revelation of Jesus is clearest in what it illuminates, and where do you feel the most ambiguity or uncertainty?

2

The End of Occupation

A Bigger Gospel

CRIME AND PUNISHMENT

Jesus saves. Sometimes words start to travel together like *avocado* and *toast*. If *Jesus* is a one-word descriptor of God, *saves* is the most common single word used to summarize his project. But of course, bumper-sticker-sized gospels suggest follow-up questions. Like, "Jesus saves from what, exactly?"

Many people today, churchgoers and not, have the impression that the primary Christian answer is "A scary God." To be clear, this is not the actual doctrine of any Christian tradition of which I am aware, any more than sixteenth-century Catholic doctrine professed salvation by works. The trouble is, gaps have a way of opening between the nuanced distinctions of specialist God-talk and what comes out on the far end of long games of religious telephone.

Perhaps at some point you encountered a summary version of the Jesus story that sounded something like this: Human beings are sinful. We've rebelled, broken God's law, done some really bad stuff. God is unhappy about this. Our bad behavior has driven a wedge between us and a perfect God. We are separated from God and awaiting the dreadful punishment that justice demands. But Jesus steps in, pays the penalty (or takes the punishment) for us, and satisfies God on our behalf. Now we can be forgiven and go to heaven when we die.

As this is one of the most common versions of the Jesus story heard in the West over the past few centuries, it's worth pausing for a moment to consider its merits.

As an empirical matter, the existence of sin is hard to deny. We humans do some messed up stuff, to ourselves and to each other, to the planet and animal kingdom; the whole world bears the scars. We would hardly expect a loving God to be delighted about the harm we cause. The idea of sin "separating" us from God sounds cruel if you picture God as a mother snapping, "No dirty fingers near my silk blouse!" But it rings differently if you imagine her saying, "This house is not the place for you if you insist on holding on to your poisonous viper collection." We might not think we personally have done something bad enough to deserve dreadful punishment, but most of us can think of a politician who has. And in our most honest moments, we might admit we're not that great at estimating how much damage to others, near and across the globe, we ourselves have done.

Metaphors of wrath and punishment appear in early Christian writings for a reason. Few people really want a God who is just "cool" with racism or child abuse or gang violence.

These metaphors take seriously the depths of wrong we do to one another and creation. They acknowledge the legitimate need for an accounting of complicity with injustice. They place God in the righteous company of truth-tellers, right-makers, and defenders of the vulnerable.

Such metaphors also speak to the crushing shame we feel when we begin to face our role in injustices and in harms that we cannot undo. Jesus appears in this picture like a president or king who stands up before the world and takes responsibility for the sins of his people, bearing their shame, owning their wrongs, and offering reparations. Jesus is one of us, the heir of Israel's royal line and representative of all humanity. This gives him the right to represent us in any court, to own the truth and accept on our behalf the justice of the attendant consequences.

THE WRATHFUL RESCUE

Yet every metaphor has its limit, a breaking point where comparison ceases to hold. For this reason, metaphors that become isolated from a larger story are particularly vulnerable to misunderstanding and distortion. This is precisely what has happened in recent centuries as many communities doubled down on just one portion of the early Christian conversation about what Jesus accomplished. Hearing metaphors of crime and punishment in isolation, many people are left with an uneasy impression that in the court of justice, God and Jesus play for different teams.

Jesus is the one you throw around a baseball with. God is the one you call to bring the bat when somebody keys your car. We can laugh, but we all know there's a disturbing truth to this understanding. There's something unsettling about this image of God, which haunts our dreams. God is the fierce judge in the sky, the threat hanging over the cosmos to ensure better behavior. God's basic feeling toward us, we can't help but suspect, is anger or disappointment. Either God is eager to give us a beating until Jesus intervenes, throwing himself in front of us. Or God is perplexingly bound to some abstract sentencing rules that God must satisfy, even against God's own better judgment.

What makes this whole picture so problematic is not that we don't *like* this image of God. Something can be unpleasant but also true—like the presence of mites on your eyelashes. The real problem is that Christianity is based on the foundational conviction that Jesus *is the very image of God.* Jesus, who became popularly known as "a friend of sinners" and who publicly ate with prostitutes and local mobsters (also known as tax collectors). Jesus, who said "Let the one without sin cast the first stone," then refused to cast one himself as the only person qualified. This is the one sent to reveal what God is really like.

Jesus said, "The Son can't do anything by himself except what he sees the Father doing. Whatever the Father does, the Son does likewise" (John 5:19). If Jesus eats with sinners, it's because he's seen God do it. If Jesus disarms the rocks, it's because that's what God desires.

Whatever problem Jesus came to solve could not be a problem with God, because God's the one who sent him to solve it. God is the one who in Jesus is cozying up with criminals, telling them they are forgiven and loved. There might be no vipers allowed in the house of God. But that doesn't mean God wouldn't jump in the middle of a snake pit to pull the rest of us out. If there is a hammer hanging over humanity's collective head—and Jesus clearly believes that there is—God is not the one holding it. God is the one initiating and bearing the costs of the rescue mission.

All this suggests that our metaphors of crime and punishment, while insightful, must be interpreted within the frame of a much larger story. A story in which God and Jesus play for the same side, fighting world-ending forces of destruction. The moment we saw Jesus, we knew that God was all-the-way-in, tear-God's-own-heart-out for us. God is not our problem. But it's clear we still have one. How do I know that? Check out the news.

THE AGE OF DUMPSTER FIRES

In the world outside the church, most people aren't lying awake worried about the wrath of God these days. Any private shame or guilt we carry is managed with the help of a trained therapist—or with the more economical aid of social media reminding us how many people out there are much, much worse than we are. But that doesn't mean there aren't plenty of other things keeping everyone awake at night.

There have been brief points in history when specific groups of people (the privileged sort) have gotten quite optimistic about the future. Maybe, they've thought, human beings will just slowly get smarter and better until we finally build utopia. Then a dreadful war breaks out and annihilates such a delusion. Evil is like a decapitated snake that just keeps on growing new heads. Old prejudices pop up from where we buried them, like zombies. Greed never even does us the courtesy of pretending to lie down. A reliable rule of technological advance is that human ingenuity will always outpace the speed of human moral discernment.

We have increased crop yields dramatically, yet somehow people are still starving. Human-caused climate change is turning forests into deserts and burying whole islands. Repressive governments multiply. Misinformation fuels genocides. To the threat of nuclear and chemical weapons we've added biological warfare. Not to mention the lingering question of whether we'll be destroyed by AI we invented to make paper clips more cheaply. In the meantime, while the robots are still working out their plans, socially alienated young men in prosperous countries continue shooting up schools.

Never mind the disasters totally out of our control—meteor strikes, plagues, freak storms, and the like. The greatest threats the world faces are of our own making, and there's no sign of a growing human capacity to get the situation under control. In such a vast universe, many scientists and philosophers have wondered, shouldn't life be more common? How is it we've not been contacted by a more advanced civilization? The jury is out. Maybe life is quite rare. Or maybe "civilization" makes a habit of ending itself not long after it figures out how to make things that go boom.

Is it any wonder so many are walking around with the sense that we are doomed? Anxiety and depression seem to be reaching all-time highs, especially among the young. There are just so many things that can fall apart and so little reason to think we will pull it together. Nihilism and despair seem almost reasonable responses to such realities.

There are still a few wild optimists among us—mostly working in Silicon Valley—who are convinced that we are one great app or invention away from solving all our problems. But an honest historian must admit the track record here is mixed at best. The same technology that largely ended world wars may one bad day abruptly end the world. The same social media that brought the globe together has perhaps irreparably divided it.

Then there are the activists, the true believers, the prophets among us, sowing blood and sweat into human dreams of something better. They are shouting warnings and ideas at the top of their lungs, but the sound seems largely lost in the vacuum of space. Everyone else is just too preoccupied trying to make it through the school pickup line. For some, bitterness and cynicism slowly strangle out their passion. For others, rage and a sense of righteous clarity start to justify hatred and physical violence.

In short, humanity's mental health seems in a rather dire state, to say nothing of our actual prospects. The apocalyptic clock seems stuck at one minute to midnight. One day we will outrun our luck. There's no denying that we need saving. But there's little sign of where help might come from.

REDISCOVERY

FOUNDING A NATION

When Jesus' biographers want to sum up his public ministry and message, they have a go-to description: "Jesus came into Galilee announcing God's good news, saying, 'Now is the time! Here comes God's kingdom! Change your hearts and lives, and trust this good news!" (Mark 1:14–15). Don't let the word *God* conjure otherworldly visions of castles floating in the clouds. The operative word for Jesus' first audience was *kingdom*. These were people who lived beneath an oppressive occupation, who'd lost control of their country. When they heard someone call for the inauguration of a new political order, they took it literally. To their ears, this Jesus from Nazareth was promoting the establishment of a new government.

A kingdom is a particular form of government where one person's will holds ultimate sway. If the king wants war, he'll get it. The same if he wants to declare French Fry Friday an official holiday. Ancient people had plenty of experience with the whims of rulers who used taxpayer money to build giant statues of themselves or who ordered the murder of dozens of babies on the fear that one of those infants might one day steal their job (see Matthew 2).

But Jesus defines the kingdom he's talking about as ruled by God. Enough with petty tyrants and fat cats living off the sweat of underlings. God is finally stepping in, taking over the government, founding a new nation. A place where God, not Pharaoh or Caesar, not a mob or a lobbyist-hijacked congress, will get what God wants.

Jesus' words and his actions make it clear why the founding of a nation under God is great news for (almost) all people. God is a lover of mercy, slow to anger and quick to forgive. God identifies with the poor and feeds the birds. God is swift in establishing justice and rectifying wrongs. God fiercely guards the well-being of children. God values and cultivates flowers. God will not rest while even one person is cold or hungry or lost. People have died by the millions for the dream of countries that promise far less than this.

The obvious question is when and where this great new nation is beginning. The "kingdom of heaven" language associated with Jesus has caused some today to imagine that Jesus was speaking of Disneyland-in-the-Sky, a better place off in the distance where you go when you die. But Jesus tells his neighbors this kingdom is *at hand*. He's not here to spark daydreams of Someday. His big news is that the revolution is starting *now*. God is acting on the plain of history. According to Jesus, everybody in earshot should get prepared, because this thing is about to go down.

By definition, heaven is the place where God's will is always enacted. Jesus tells his followers, "Pray, 'Your kingdom come, your will be done *on earth* as it is heaven.'" This is the project he's initiating. Jesus is recruiting a people to live under God's good rule *here and now*. The seeds of heaven are being planted in the soil of the earth. Jesus says, the ideals and experiences of heaven, which once felt so far away, are coming soon to a neighborhood near you.

KINGDOM MISUNDERSTANDINGS

The first-century people who first hear Jesus' words are ripe for talk of revolution. They are desperate to live under God's just rule rather than some foreign emperor and a bunch of corrupt local overlords. This talk of a new nation is music to their ears. When they hear Jesus say "Right here and right now," they're ready to rally to the call. However, it turns out they have a few critical misunderstandings about the nature of the project.

Kingdoms are typically understood as discrete territories that can be designated on a map. They're under unified control. They're defendable by arms. They have borders that are held against opposing claims and rulers. This is the kind of kingdom Israel once had when famous kings like David beat back the Philistines. Everybody assumes that David's charismatic descendant Jesus is about a similar project. He will recruit an army, drive out the Romans, reestablish national borders, consolidate control, and set up a formal government. Even Jesus' twelve closest followers share these assumptions, going so far as to squabble over which of them will be chief of staff in the new administration (Mark 10:35–45).

In this respect, Jesus is an utter failure and disappointment to most who initially admired him. He arrives at the capital city, and they do their part in declaring him king. But when the moment comes to ignite the revolution, Jesus steps down instead of up. He rallies no troops. He starts no fights. He takes no land. He topples no despots. Disappointed, Jesus' fan base turns on him, chanting for his death. Jesus is crucified under the mocking title "the king of the Jews"—another lying, useless politician who promised the world and delivered nothing.

Something has clearly been lost in translation between Jesus' stated intentions and the expectations of his fans. But what?

Contrary to what many today are told, Jesus did not suggest that the kingdom he came to bring was only or primarily an inward reality, the spiritual reign of God within an individual heart alone. Jesus spoke constantly about social arrangements and public realities—about justice and debts and dinner parties and dealing with enemies. The kingdom that Jesus had in mind was a political and social entity. However, this kingdom also operated with critically different parameters from others.

To begin with, the kingdom of God that Jesus spoke of has a different relationship with land. Rather than control a limited piece of earth with defensible borders, this kingdom spreads by way of outposts. Wherever its citizens set up tents, there it will claim ground. There are no borders or places where it can be shut out. It expands across the globe, occupying territory, not through force of arms but through voluntary recruitment.

The kingdom of God also has a different sort of citizenry. The people of this new nation do not live in one geographic spot, nor do they share an ethnicity or language. Its citizenship roster is open. People from every nation can transfer in, pledge allegiance, and submit to Jesus' rule. Wherever they do this, even in groups of two or three, an outpost of God's kingdom emerges—a spot of earth where God's will is done as it is in heaven.

Every kingdom must have laws. God's new, dispersed kingdom has one: the law of self-giving love. Love God with all your being; love your neighbor as yourself (Matthew 22:37–39). According to Jesus, that pretty much sums it up. This single, two-part universal law undergirds all the others, which are locally contextualized expressions of it. In this system there are no outdated rules or rigid legalism. Where true love is enacted, the King's will is accomplished.

Kingdoms are communities with cultures. Many of Jesus' teachings describe the kind of culture that will mark God's new society. It is a culture of hospitality, generosity, open-handed sharing. This culture practices justice but loves mercy most. Leadership is recognized by sacrifice and humble service. Truth is spoken, always, and all things are done in daylight. These are visible signs that will distinguish an outpost of God's rule from other kingdoms that surround it on every side.

GOD AND THE DUMPSTER FIRES

The name that Jesus was given at birth literally means "God saves." From the first word, Jesus' story was understood in a salvation frame. The God who once heard the cries of a group of slaves in Egypt has heard the cries of enslaved people everywhere else. God has heard the cries of pain caused by injustice and occupation. The abuse. The addiction. The loneliness. The prejudice. The fear. The shame. God has heard the cries and been moved by them. And God has conceived a rescue plan.

The heart of this rescue plan was not an alien abduction nor a vaguely grounded promise to someday evacuate all good souls from the mess. Such a rescue plan was far too small for a God who loved a world. And God loves the world. God loves the loamy smell of the desert after rain. The komondor dog that looks like a mop. The droopy deep-sea blobfish. The song of wind in pines. The burning gases of deep space. God loves human bodies. The rolls of baby thighs. The calluses of working hands.

God loves people. The injured ones lying in the ditch. The good ones who stop to help. The bad ones who put this guy in that ditch or assume he deserves to be there. The angry ones who barricade the road in protest of this treatment. The fearful ones who cross to the opposite side. The distracted ones who walk on by without noticing. God has come for all of them, the entire motley cast and crew of history's drama. God's rescue plan is to save all of them, to save all creation, to reclaim its design. God's plan is to "heaven" the earth, to close the gap, to make the two realms one—a single place where God's good, just will is always done (see Revelation 21–22).

REDISCOVERY #2:

Salvation encompasses the setting right
of all things, on earth as it is in heaven.

The first rediscovery of a Jesus-looking God leads naturally to the second—a rediscovery of what a God like Jesus means for the world. God is not passively content to watch the world burn. The one who created the cosmos for good has always had a stake in its destiny. God is not scrapping this project because of too many errors.[1]

Salvation involves a comprehensive rescue of humanity and all creation from everything that distorts its design. It includes

---

1. The Bible's famous story of Noah and his rainbow in Genesis 6–9 is a reminder of God's promise not to despair and toss the whole thing in the dust bin.

the establishment of a new world where God's good will gets done, the formation of a borderless land where people live together in every effervescent shade of justice and pattern of peace. It is a liberation of all creation for its glorious destiny.

This is God's big project, which Jesus declares is beginning right here, right now, with him. The question that remains is how exactly this outcome will be accomplished.

TURNING THE TIDE

In many ways, it's as important to understand how this rescue does *not* work as it is to understand how it does. Jesus does not come along just to save us from our ignorance, as if the only thing standing between us and a perfect world is a bit of knowledge about how we should really be behaving. Knowing better has not put Taco Bell out of business nor eliminated texting while driving. God's big plan is not just to fill us all in on a better way of living, after which we'll cry "Of course!" and pull ourselves and the world back together.

Our human fears and prejudices have created massive, destructive weather systems. A fluttering wing of greed stirs up storms around the globe. We take the first bite of poison apple willingly, convinced one little taste couldn't hurt us. But one taste can often be all it takes to form a deadly addiction. The small bias in us fans the spark in another, and soon a societal forest fire is raging.

The early Jesus followers had a term to describe the invisible forces that cause destruction to mysteriously grow like a snowball rolling downhill, accelerating exponentially past what we foresee. They called them "the powers." The energy that somehow shifts a crowd into a mob. The gravity that pulls corporate structures toward corruption. The voice in our head that whispers we are worthless. The self-destructive impulse that compels us to shoot our own foot. There is more going on in the world than meets the eye. The cosmos is composed of more than only visible matter; it is spiritually alive. There are spiritual currents moving through the world, pulling us like riptides.

It's sort of like all of us, for various reasons, have been making tiny chips in a massive dam. The many chips form larger cracks, and eventually the dam collapses. Now we and creation are being swept along in a raging torrent of unleashed destructive powers. This is not a problem that can be solved with clever engineering—not when all the engineers are also swirling out of control. The only hope is help that comes from beyond.

Enter Jesus. In Jesus, God jumps into the twisting current with us. The tidal wave of evil we unleashed lands directly on him. And it breaks his body, just as it breaks the rest of us vulnerable humans. But Jesus is not just like the rest of us. He also carries within him the power, the presence, the authority of God. So something else happens when the wave of chaos lands on him—it breaks him, but it also breaks itself.

THE END OF OCCUPATION

The early church described this operation through the metaphor of something akin to a hostage rescue. God made the world for good, but it is currently occupied by unseen forces of resistance, led by a tyrant on a mission to steal, kill, and destroy (John 10:10).

The story is complicated because we humans aren't just helpless victims. We are players too. We are easily convinced that we can run the world without God's help. The tyrant encourages this delusion, using our arrogance to take us captive. We have become trapped by our own fears and appetites and egos. We've been deceived, seduced, or intimidated into service to our captor. Meanwhile, God is on a mission to depose the tyrant, to disrupt the reign of evil, to set us and creation with us free so we can become truly ourselves. God launches Operation Incarnation—a daring plan to send God's Son in disguise behind enemy lines.

In his ministry, Jesus casts out demons, heals the sick, and confronts corrupt power—pushing back at evil. But he never loses sight of the fact that he is a battlefield doctor, treating symptoms while a war still rages. Jesus has come into the world not just to bind up endless wounds but to win the war itself. He has come to deal with the tyrant, dethrone the power of evil, and free the prisoners of war.

The moment that Jesus steps onto the field, he has evil's full attention. Wherever he goes, the forces of hatred and chaos recognize him. They cannot guess his game, but it is clear that his human "condition" makes him vulnerable. Evil's first play is to tempt Jesus with the fears and ego-feeding promises that worked on all the others. But Jesus sees through it and calls out the lies. So evil eventually forsakes subtlety and stages a frontal attack. God's opposition rallies a deadly alliance of greedy religious leaders, political leaders with power to protect, and ordinary people with their own resentments and desires.

Jesus' death is the culmination of the whole disastrous unraveling of human history. All the fear and greed and injustice and violence we harbored, every lie the tyrant told, led us here—to the mob-driven murder of God. Humanity releases the world-ending atomic bomb of evil. And Jesus throws himself on it, absorbs the force in his own body. He dies. The opposition celebrates, believing they have won.

But it turns out that evil has overplayed its hand, wildly underestimating the power of God. The tyrant didn't guess God's secret plan—to destroy the power of death by dying (Hebrews 2:14).

What occurs next ancient Christians grandly named "the ravaging of hell." Jesus dies and falls to rock bottom with us. He enters the grave, the final place where the tyrant holds his captives. When Jesus gets there, he uses his own hands to rip the bars off the cells.

Jesus is one of us, but he is also Son of God. Evil simply didn't get what it was messing with. When it swallowed him, it swallowed the power that ignited a hundred billion suns. It took that love, that light, that life, that fire into the very heart of darkness. And the darkness was no match for it. When God calls Jesus' name, no prison can hold him. The doors blow off the castle. Jesus starts going person to person, to captives dead and captives alive, breaking off chains and calling everyone to follow him out, into a better land of freedom.

The early church summed it up like this: "[Jesus] rescued us from the control of darkness and transferred us into the kingdom of the Son he loves. He set us free through the Son and forgave our sins" (Colossians 1:13–14). Jesus conducted the greatest prison break in history. That break is still going on. Evil's estate is being plundered; God is taking back every single stolen good and emptying the dungeon (Mark 3:26–27). And God is determined not to leave a single thing behind.

TRANSFORMATION

THE FUTURE OF EVERYTHING

The story of Jesus is big. Really big. Cosmic-sized. It's the story of a battle between good and evil. Life and death. Truth and deception. Coherence and chaos. It's a story of planetary occupation and of divine resistance. It's the story of a triune God hatching a daring rescue scheme in which the risk, the cost, the sacrifice is taken from heaven's own accounts.

This story is rooted not in God's disappointment or disgust but in God's magnificent obsession with a world God can't let go. The existence of the cosmos is itself a free expression of God's overflowing love and longing for a place to pour it. The redemption of the cosmos issues from this same source. To speak of God's wrath is to speak of God's determined opposition to all the divides and distortions—God's chain-breaking, right-making energy directed toward healing and freedom.

Humanity was designed for a unique role in creation—to lead, under God's oversight, in service of creation. The world's destiny is bound to ours; where we go, it soon follows. When we unleashed the dam, creation got swept downriver with us. This is why God's rescue plan ultimately starts with humans. Not because we are the only ones loved in this glorious creation. But because we are the door to the rest. God comes for us with the intent of taking all (Romans 8:19–21). This is the scale of the world-redeeming story now unfolding.

The endgame of God's mission has never been creation's destruction but its reclamation. God's dream, which the start of the Bible depicts as an idyllic garden, is reimagined at the end of the Bible as a garden city. Here the artistry of God and the artistry of humans, God's small image-bearers, intermingle and intertwine. What emerges from this cooperative creative effort is a landscape of beauty and universal flourishing. This is earth as heaven. This is humanity, rescued and freed and finally developing as students of the Master Artist. This is the rest of creation, caught up with us in our rise.

The story of Jesus requires, thank God (really), not a shred of actual optimism. You don't have to believe that self-help books will solve any of your problems. You don't have to trust technological breakthrough. You don't have to blindly hope that human beings turn out to be better than they seem. God loves the world without delusion. So can we. The disease may have progressed well past our ability to cure it. But it is not beyond the curative power of the one who created it to start with. Jesus' announcement was good news because it was the announcement of help come from outside the chaos, the arrival of one come to do for us what we could never do for ourselves. A plummeting planet is being caught by hands strong and soft enough to break its fall without shattering it.

LEAVING THE STRONGHOLD

In the war for the world, the tide has been turned. But let's be real—it doesn't always feel that way.

In war, there is often a rather strange period near the end when the outcome has been decided but still must be carried out into the field. This is how the early Christians came to understand our present circumstances. The decisive battle has already been fought. Jesus won; the enemy knows it. But evil, though doomed, has not yet laid down its arms.

An ancient Christian text called Revelation pictures evil, the fallen tyrant, as a rampaging dragon (Revelation 12). The dragon knows he has taken a mortal wound. His reign is over; he's bleeding out. And he is real ticked off about it. After all, Jesus didn't just win—he humiliated the powers of evil, exposed their hollowness and weakness for the universe to see (Colossians 2:15).

A dying dragon can still rage and cause pain. But he can't reverse the damage done to him and his armies. He can try to steal and kill. But he can no longer hold anything he claims. He can't put the bars back on the dungeon. He can't rebuild the stronghold's doors. There's really only one move he has left—to lie to people and convince them not to leave their open cell.

Now this is where things get really interesting. A person can be free, but not realize it—as occurred after the American Civil War when Texas slaveholders hid the news of emancipation. It's also possible for a person to be free, but not live like it. A person can be free, but not yet understand what freedom really means. The rescue is enacted, but it has to be both announced and embraced.

Jesus saves. In one sense, it happens the moment the death blow to evil is dealt. But in another sense, this rescue is an ongoing project that demands participation. It's the work of a lifetime to let Jesus draw us to the prison exit. It's perhaps the work of an eternity to learn how to live truly free. The journey doesn't always advance in one direction. Sometimes we return to the cell. Perhaps because the cell is familiar. Perhaps because a cage can often feel less dangerous than freedom. Liberation is a gift, but it isn't for cowards, and it generally takes a long time to unwrap.

That's okay. God is famously patient. With the death of death secured, God has a lot of time to work with. The reality of the rescue is not altered by the speed of the exit. The bars are off, and that's the most important thing. God will come. And come. And come. And come again. And say, "Follow me out to somewhere better." How many times? Infinity times infinity, Jesus teases his followers. In other words, as many times as it takes.

There is also a role in this story for us to play in the rescue of others. Those exiting the prison can rally other captives. There's no need to claim to have the answers or know more than we do. We don't even have to pretend we know exactly where the exit lies. It's enough to know that the doors are open. It's enough to say, "I've met somebody who has been outside. He says he knows the way to get there. Let's follow him together and see where we end up."

LIVING WITH A DYING DRAGON

Jesus' grand announcement was a rescue of this earth, not planetary evacuation. His endgame was the establishment of a new nation of free human citizens, not a plan to sew wings on human backs and increase heaven's angel collection. But all this doesn't mean that questions of the afterlife are not urgently relevant to Jesus' message.

The afterlife was a hotly contested question in Jesus' day, and Jesus clearly and explicitly came down on one side of the debate. All people are alive to God (Luke 20:38). Death is a bend in the road beyond which we cannot yet see clearly. But it is certainly not the end of the human story. God has made us for forever.

Every road has two ditches. If one common distortion of the Jesus story is to make it all future and otherworldly, another is to make its promises all present. Language of "building God's kingdom" can make it sound like the future's arrival is a human infrastructure project—massive, slow, laborious but doable with enough time and elbow grease.

There was no naïve optimism in the teachings of Jesus. Precisely because he takes the problem of evil so seriously, Jesus can fully calculate the cost of overcoming it. Jesus notes many times that he is sending his followers out in a vulnerable position. God's rescued citizens are dispersed in outposts across the world, in places where God's justice is not currently enacted. The opposition is still on the field and looking to kick in some teeth—especially of those bearing more than a passing family resemblance to the One who sealed its doom.

To live out an alternative culture under a different authority is not always popular. To live free in a world of captives suffering from Stockholm syndrome is not always safe. Jesus' followers would be—and are—seen as a threat to the status quo and the powers that benefit from it. To make things even more complicated, Jesus disarms his citizens before sending them out into this uncertain field. They are told to win friends, love enemies, and overcome evil with good. To accept the single law of the new nation—loving as God does—is to embrace the vulnerability that Jesus himself modeled on the cross (more on this in chapter 7). It's to accept the real possibility that things may go very wrong for a while.

This is why the resurrection of Jesus is not incidental to his message but essential to it. It is the promise of a second act that breathes courage into controversial loyalties and gracefully defiant living. Hope is the only fuel on which indiscriminate love can run. Resurrection is utterly crucial to the full arc of God's justice. The dragon can rage and hiss and bite. He can even maim and kill. But sooner or later, one way or another, Jesus' followers will crush the winged serpent's head, just as Jesus did (Luke 10:18–20). It's only a matter of time.

Nothing can be lost that will not be restored. Nothing can be spent that will not be returned. Nothing can be broken that will not be mended. Nothing can be bent that will not be straightened. Nothing can die that will not live again. We are destined for forever, with God and with each other, as part of a renewed creation. This assurance produces a revolutionary change in the calculus of risk and sacrifice.

The first Christians were not always popular among their neighbors. They were seen as weird, even antisocial, for their countercultural behavior. Their morality looked foreign and sometimes off-putting. But there was one thing that nobody seemed to deny—these people were brave. Nothing could stop them from sharing, from speaking, from serving, from loving. Fear no longer owned their stories.

Jesus saves. Once you know this, once you really grasp that there's no way to lose, that's the moment you become a real hell-shaker—an unleashed, darkness-piercing dragon-stomper.

CONVERSATION STARTERS

1. What practical difference does it make if we view the Jesus story as fundamentally a rescue story as opposed to a self-help story?
2. What role does Jesus play in God's plan to rescue creation?
3. What role do you think we play in this rescue story? What are our responsibilities? What are our limitations?
4. What do you think makes the kingdom of God different from other kingdoms or nations we are familiar with?
5. What would change about the story and message of Jesus without the resurrection?

Apprenticing Freedom

A New Kind of Human

DILEMMA

THE LOW SIDE OF AVERAGE

God is as gracious and good as Jesus is. God is heavening earth. So far it sounds like a pretty good story. We'd all be happy if it were true. Yet a critical problem is eroding the story's credibility: lots of Christians are jerks.

There's no point in denying it. We all know these people. They read their Bible every day. They attend church every week. Every December they're primed for a public fight over the meaning of Christmas. But they're also stingy with their employees. Controlling of their families. Dismissive of the struggles of their neighbors. Vicious with their children's teachers. It seems like Christianity has somehow mysteriously made them *worse*.

To be fair, these terrible Christians are (arguably) a minority. Most of the time, you can't tell the difference between a Christian and anybody else, except when they flood the restaurants at precisely two minutes after noon on Sundays. They drive the same cars. They live in the same houses. They watch the same amount of TV. They consume the same quantities of fossil fuels and alcohol. They have the same average marriage success rate. They rant roughly the average amount on social media. They cause an average amount of trouble for the coach of the Little League team.

None of this will likely surprise you if you've spent much time around a church. But you can see why, from the outside, it might feel like an odd disconnect. Here you have the grand story of a loving God waging cosmic battle to overcome evil and rescue the world for good. Told by people who look and live much like everybody else, except slightly judgy-er.

There's considerable diversity in moral beliefs among Christians—much more than many would suppose or prefer. But there's also a non-trivial list of things on which nearly all Jesus followers agree: cheating is bad; caring for the poor is good; you should love your neighbors of every race; it's important to tell the truth. Most Christian churches teach these things—if with varying degrees of emphasis. Most self-described Christians believe them—if with some quibbles on the language and methods. If the few billion Christians out there actually did only the most obvious things we almost all agree upon, the world would undoubtedly be a much better place.

But we don't. At least not on a wide enough scale for Christians to gain a reputation for an overall average of difference. Quantity of cross-marked T-shirts does not reliably predict quality of cross-marked behavior. Why not? If God's big plan is transforming the world through Jesus, it's kind of worrying that so many Jesus people appear so little altered.

THE GREAT DISCONNECT

This gaping disconnect between God's big story and the real-world activity (or lack thereof) of the story's adherents might be traced to at least three separate but related causes. First, if you start with a distorted picture of God, your behavior is almost guaranteed to mirror the distortions. This is a natural consequence of the themes we've been discussing over the previous two chapters. Views of God unanchored by the revelation of Jesus lead many to mistake legalism for righteousness, or fairness for justice, or freedom for license.

The problem in these cases is not that people are failing to be transformed; the problem is they are being transformed into a false image. They are becoming like the god they worship; that god simply isn't Jesus-shaped. Their understanding of God's character, God's values, and God's priorities has not yet been redefined by the message and methods of Jesus himself.

The second problem is that, as we're all painfully aware, it's possible to have the right ideas and intentions but lack the capacity to follow them through. I am properly persuaded that brussels sprouts are better than nachos as contributors to positive life outcomes. That doesn't mean I'll successfully find strength to choose them when facing a bowl of queso. We might aspire to every Jesus-shaped ideal but still feel too empty, afraid, or powerless to choose them (more on this in chapter 6).

But there is an even more basic problem still: motivation. Change is hard, and we're not always eager to do it. It can be painful to grow, to alter our patterns and perspectives, to leave things behind. Sometimes we'd just as soon stay where we are.

The motivational difficulty manifested by modern Christianity can be traced directly to what many have been told about the kingdom of heaven opt-in process. According to many modern Jesus-recruiters, the process of opting in to a better future has a few key steps: believe that Jesus is the rescuer, ask his forgiveness, and invite him "into your heart"—a somewhat ambiguous metaphor that seems to imply emotional attachment. Steps 1-2-3, and the process is done. Your heavenly bus ticket is secured; you're as saved as you're going to get.

In defense of the earnest recruiters, this simple narration has the significant merit of keeping the focus on God as willing rescuer, not on you scraping together moral quarters to earn your seat on the bus. During the last reformation, the revelation of salvation as the free gift of God was a critical rediscovery, correcting widespread misperceptions that one could or *must* somehow buy a ticket into God's good graces. Even today, five centuries later, many still believe that God's forgiveness and affection belong only to those who consistently fulfill their weekly good deeds quota.

Most well-intended Christian recruiters also attempt to make clear there's a second stage to the journey: once you've been rescued, you're supposed to use your newfound freedom to start living differently. The trouble is, the connection between "Salvation: The Movie" and its lesser-known sequel "Life Change" is weak enough that a lot falls between the cracks. Love of neighbor hooks onto the divine rescue story a bit like an optional car accessory. Everyone gets that it's better if you have it. But either way the car still drives, still gets you to the destination.

"Jesus is my Savior," Christians like to say. We get that we should let him be Lord too. After all, we kind of owe him. The gift might be free, but a decent preacher can probably leverage some guilt about our failure to reciprocate. Sort of like when that charity sent you the free address labels and you had to make a donation in return to feel good about yourself.

However, guilt has serious limits as a motivational tool, tending as it does to fade the moment those nice labels get tucked out of view or a more tempting use for funds presents itself (Taylor Swift tickets, anyone?). The reality is that for most of us, any brief reminders of "higher causes" are swamped by waves of daily distractions and stimulation. It's estimated that most of us are exposed to more than four thousand advertisements per day. This means a half-hour weekly sermon is up against an average of eighteen hours of television viewing and twenty-eight thousand ads selling us alternative stories of the true, the good, the beautiful, the possible. Is it really any wonder if the latter has more power to shape imagination and desire?

It's not that we don't know that transformation is important. We just hope it will be easier tomorrow. Or the day after. Or maybe after death, where God will probably have invented some accelerated method for human improvement, a moral microwave where patience can be baked in six minutes or less.

BECOMING TOGETHER

Concern for personal transformation is hardly exclusive to religion. Transformation is a booming global industry. Everyone from plastic surgeons and fitness instructors to personal coaches and therapists promises to unleash "a better you." Enormous quantities of time and resources are devoted to convincing us of the need to find our authentic self—and then to subtly improve it.

This cultural drive for personal change is fueled by a particular story of the world: Beneath the weight of societal expectations and family pressures and the burdens of late capitalism lies a true version of you—unconstrained and self-defined and primed for living your own bliss. Our highest obligation is to unburden and release that more authentic self. To get there we must work together to rid ourselves of all obligations, constraints, and categories and to maximize our individual freedom. The only limit is the point at which our authentic expression impinges on somebody else's.

To be clear, this is a salvation story, just like the Christian story. It is also a serious moral project, not to be taken lightly. This project has arisen in significant part as a response to a sordid and frequently violent history of religion confining people to tiny boxes in the name of God. For centuries, the baseline assumption of the so-called Christian West was that there was only one way to be properly human—a way which, coincidentally, featured white European table manners and inexplicable fondness for hoop skirts. "God" all too easily becomes a convenient defense for cultural preferences of social order. When faith and culture travel together, it's rarely clear which one is driving. People have also noticed over time that the size and shape of boxes in which they're pressured to reside tend to be defined by whoever has most social power.

It's no wonder that centuries of small-mindedness and systematic diminishment of entire groups of people has provoked a fierce rebellion. In the best cases, discovery of the many diversities of human individuals and cultures evokes greater playfulness and spaciousness for all. It invites the recovery of perhaps the most ancient human virtue: hospitality, the practice of making room for the other without trying to re-create them in the image of ourselves. More than that, it provides an opportunity to celebrate many forms of goodness and beauty—to embrace, a religious person might suggest, a fuller image of God.

Nevertheless, the modern secular salvation story has its own distinct weaknesses.

To begin with, becoming an authentic self is much more complex than it first appears. Ditching all categories, all expectations, all obligations, and starting from scratch, the true self can be hard to find—a bit like searching for a specific sea sponge in the middle of the ocean. How do you know which sponge is the truest you when there are so many possibilities out there? How do you even know where to look? The search can feel paralyzing, especially to the young. The pursuit can be so exhausting and endless that little energy remains to turn outward toward the world or toward true encounter with others.

Identity is also slippery; just when you think you've caught it, it can slide between your hands. Even those who see clearly who they want to be can find the process of getting there elusive. You might want to be courageous, bold, a prophetic voice of truth. You might accurately sense the seeds of all these things within you. Yet shadowed fears and hidden traumas, wordless insecurities and unnamed inhibitions, rob the soil of nutrients and stifle the seeds' growth. Internal resistance is as real as the external sort and often harder to confront. Becoming a person is more difficult than it seems from the outside.

In a different respect, many are also slowly awakening to the fact that personal freedom is a true but rather narrow good. It feels nice to be unconstrained and "real"—especially when you've been locked in an ill-fitting box. It feels liberating to be relieved of the burden of judging other peoples' selfhood. But sooner or later, many of us start to feel that something is still missing. We want to be our authentic selves. But not on desert islands or in tiny enclaves of people just like us. We want to be free. But we also want connection, security, belonging. To be understood. To be part of a team. To find purpose in relation to others.

It turns out that most of us don't just want to self-express without interference. We want to be part of a larger society capable of recognizing beauty and goodness. We want a community that builds things together that are better than what any faction of us could manufacture alone. We might even want a few things that mar the fabric of communal goodness to be considered out of bounds.

At the point of this collective good for which we scarcely have a name, our modern transformation toolbox starts to fail. These modern tools have been crafted to reveal and refine an authentic individual person. But they were not designed to shape diversities into a cohesive and interdependent whole. They excel at creating a *me* and a *you*, but they flounder at the task of creating an integrated *us*.

The result is a world where, justified or not, nearly everyone seems to end up feeling that they are in some way "outside" the ambiguous collective. The strongest bonds often form in bands of not-belonging. Sometimes the bonds of "outsiders" can be deeply beautiful. In other cases, however, social bonds that solidify around anger and alienation rather than shared goodness can grow both inwardly and outwardly destructive.

REDISCOVERY

THE EARLIEST MANIFESTO

The early church had a creed—a manifesto, if you will—that summed up the heart of their corporate identity. It was not a

ten-page document explicating core doctrines. It was a statement so short and simple a toddler could memorize it. A three-
word phrase (two words, if you speak Greek) that summed up
a global revolution: Jesus. Is. Lord.

Kurios Christos. Jesus is Lord. Not "God is real." Not "Jesus
is Savior"—although the early church did indeed believe that
(more on this later). Jesus is Lord. This was the world-shaking
manifesto on which the whole Christian movement was built.

"Lord" was a title commonly used in Judaism to refer to
God. In this sense, to declare "Jesus is Lord" was to express
your conviction that Jesus of Nazareth had definitively demonstrated what God is really like. There couldn't be a more radical claim in the context of first-century Judaism.

But in the context of the Roman Empire, the declaration
"Jesus is Lord" had a different, no less radical, resonance. In
this world, "Caesar is Lord" was a phrase heard on the streets
every day. It was a claim focused not so much on divinity as
on authority. Your lord was the one to whom you owed your
fealty. The one from whom you took your marching orders.

By earliest definition, to be a Christian was not to hold a
certain abstract set of beliefs about God. It was not to have
prayed a particular prayer or enacted a specific ritual. It was
certainly not to have been born in a certain culture or community. A Christian was one who acknowledged and submitted
to a particular authority. Not the emperor's. Not their local
religious leader's. Not their own. Jesus'.

DECLARATION OF ALLEGIANCE

Acknowledging Jesus as ultimate authority had both corporate
and profoundly personal dimensions. The collective implications were immediately clear and costly, because to declare
that Jesus is Lord was an unmistakably political statement

in the first century. We noted in the previous chapter that Jesus' core message—"Now is the time! Here comes God's kingdom!"—was the declaration of an inbreaking, new social reality. Jesus was founding a nation, albeit one different from the others, calling citizens together under a new rule.

The earliest disciples of Jesus understood that to be a Christian was not primarily a matter of private belief or even inward affection. It was first and foremost a designation that signaled allegiance. Baptism, the initiatory rite of the church, was a public ritual officially marking the transfer of citizenship. From this day forward, they were Jesus'. What he said, they would do. Where he led, they would follow.

This commitment was made publicly because it had to be kept publicly. Under Jesus' rule, the early Christians embraced whole new structures of life—new ways of being both individually and collectively that were instantly visible. The first Christians quickly became known for their new economic system. They didn't eliminate the notion of private property, but they no longer held their property in the same way. As needs arose, wealth was redistributed voluntarily among these Christians, resulting in a situation where none was truly poor. What belonged to one was assumed to exist for the sake of all. Neighbors watched this spectacle with suspicion but also curiosity and some envy. Some were so attracted, they chose to join the church.

The early Christians celebrated sex within the covenant of marriage. This too was far outside the norm in Caesar's world—at least for men. To some outsiders it looked prudish and restrictive. But interestingly, within this relatively constrained sexual environment, gender relationships began to look different. Single people found a place of respect. Women began to lead, a rarity at the time. People called each other "brother" and "sister"—and accepted the attendant obligations of mutual honor and care.

Under Jesus' rule, early Christians gave enemies the extra-mile treatment and refused to retaliate when persecuted. This could not have provided a more striking contrast with the brutality of the Roman emperors, who answered even a hint of threat with slaughter. When the emperor gave them to lions for their claims to live under a different authority, the Jesus people did not resist. Viewing the integrity of their living and the dignity of their dying, many of their neighbors decided to serve Lord Jesus instead of Lord Caesar.

The early Christians ate together at a diverse table—day laborers and aristocrats, Jewish fisherman and Roman soldiers, men and women, Scythians and Phoenicians, slaves and citizens. It was unheard of. It was strange. It caused all kinds of complicated problems—the sorts you'd expect when different cultures and classes begin attempting to relate outside their prescribed hierarchies. It was chaotic, often painful. Yet more and more kept deciding to give this odd new nation a look. Especially those enslaved. Especially women. Especially non-Jewish God-fearers who lingered on the margins of the synagogues.

In times of plague, Christians risked their lives to care for each other and their neighbors. When infants were abandoned outside and left to die—a common practice when their fathers wanted no more heirs—Jesus people took them in. This was being Christian. To "ask Jesus into your heart," while not technically incorrect, would likely have seemed to them a perplexingly small way to describe what they were doing. Where Jesus was Lord, the whole world was reordered. Christians lived and died every day under a new authority. No aspect of life was untransformed.

THE FIRST TRUE HUMAN

Allegiance to Jesus manifested in a communal transformation, as a new way of being *together* in the world. However, no massive social change is possible without profound change in the attitudes, desires, and daily habits of individuals. The early church was very aware of the deeply personal dimensions of this transformation. The conclusion that Jesus had definitively revealed the heart of God was coupled in the ancient church with a second, equally radical conclusion: Jesus had also definitively revealed the shape of humanity. Simply put, Jesus was the first true human.

If every computer you'd ever encountered had a virus that corrupted files, crashed its programs, and slowed its speed, how would you even guess what the device was truly capable of? In similar fashion, humanity has been disfigured by a rampant disease. Everyone you've ever met has had it. Universal human distortion had so long concealed the design that no one knew what a properly functioning human being in the image of God looked like. Then along comes Jesus, who essentially says, "Follow me, and I'll show you the shape of true humanity. Follow me, and I'll apprentice you in becoming truly human yourself."

"Lord" is a challenging title because it means acknowledging that somebody knows better than you do what you were meant to be and how you're going to get there. This can be a tough pill for modern people to swallow, especially since we'd all like to think that following our inner voice will get us where we want to go. It's hard to admit that our inner voice may not be fully reliable. It can be hard to accept the possibility there may be someone who sees us more clearly than we see ourselves—although the wise often do eventually begin to suspect that self-narration has its limits and blind spots.

When Jesus offers himself as "Lord," it is not with the goal of restriction. Jesus makes this explicit. Jesus is not Pharaoh or Caesar. He has come to release captives, not to take them. His opponents aim to steal, kill, and destroy. Jesus has come so every person may become at last fully alive (John 10:10). He has come as the Designer to reveal the real shape of the design.

Paradoxically, binding oneself to Jesus is the only sure pathway to freedom.

In practice, apprenticing in humanity with Jesus can be tricky. Jesus tells individuals who come to him to count the cost before opting in. Following him will often lead to places they would not otherwise go. There may not be room for all the baggage they'd otherwise prefer to bring along. To be free, some things must be let go or left behind. To be healed, bones must sometimes be broken to properly reset. There is no way to truly live without something for which you are willing to die.

When all you've experienced is distortion, the true shape of wholeness can be hard to believe. Hearing Jesus say to give money away can sound like deprivation or loss of safety. It's hard to imagine that giving away might lead to better relationships or less anxiety. Hearing Jesus instruct radical forgiveness can sound grossly unfair. It's hard to anticipate the relief of no record-keeping, or the reduction in our own sense of shame when we release the role of judge. Hearing Jesus teach covenant for life can sound restrictive. It's hard to conceive all the ways this commitment might lead to greater freedom and intimacy.

Among the most surprising revelations of Jesus is his statement "All who lose their lives because of me will find them" (Matthew 16:25). This is not only a promise of divine return; it is a profound insight into the nature of humanity itself. Some things resist direct pursuit; they can be found only by seeking something else. It is not in grasping our "selves" but in giving them away that we become a true self at all.

With this statement, Jesus also suggests that all our choices, all our grasping or releasing, should be made with clear perception of a longer timeline. Everything changes when the temporal frame shifts. If "you only live once," for a few short decades, it seems almost a moral obligation to get what you can while you can. If you expect to live twice, and the second time forever, the math of pleasure and planning, of waiting and foregoing, of hoping and sacrificing, changes dramatically.

What at first seems bizarre if not outright fantastical in Jesus' teachings often has a hidden logic that isn't visible until we're partway through. Our humanity is frequently found in places we aren't looking. The best thing we can do is follow someone who's seen the design specs.

If Jesus is the image of true humanity, one might suppose that those who apprentice him would become over time more and more like each other—an army of khaki-wearing clones who all love Froyo and chorale singing. However, it turns out that our common fears and hang-ups are holding us in generic parades of captives. When we are cleansed of these things, the image of God begins to shine through more brightly in all its diverse shapes and shades. As we give ourselves away for others, we discover the gifts that are in fact most uniquely ours to give.

WALKING THE WAY

It's become common in certain contexts to hear people define a Christian as one who "accepts Jesus as their personal Savior." There is absolutely no question that from the first days of Christianity, the Jesus story has been preached and understood as a rescue story. However, what has often been lost is the crucial link between salvation and lordship. For the early Christians, the ground of the story was summed up in their two-word creed: *Kurios Christos*. Jesus is Lord. This is what salvation looks like. This is the way it comes.

REDISCOVERY #3:

A Christian is one who acknowledges Jesus as Lord and follows him in life and death.

Jesus is Savior. Jesus is Lord. These two realities, these two roles, do not merely travel side by side. One is dependent on the other. Jesus saves *by becoming Lord.* This was the early Christian story. A new authority has come to town to overthrow evil and to mend what's broken. Those who submit to him, who offer him allegiance, become citizens of the nation he is starting. They are saved in becoming part of his new world that is rising.

The most influential teacher in the early church, the apostle Paul, puts it like this: "If you confess with your mouth 'Jesus is Lord' and in your heart you have faith that God raised him from the dead, you will be saved" (Romans 10:9). Notice the sequence. The rescue we are waiting for begins with an act of confession. "Confess" here is not the language of private, inward belief but a public declaration of recognition and allegiance. Salvation begins, according to Paul, the moment you choose to bind yourself under a new authority. An authority that was demonstrated, declared to the world, when God brought Jesus back from death.

Ancient Christians liked to speak of this rescue in three tenses: "We have been saved. We are being saved. And we will be saved."[1] On the one hand, the public vow of loyalty and allegiance brings an instant change in status—the past tense. You have become a citizen of the Jesus Nation, one of his people. This new identity is more defining than any other that you hold. Your fate is now bound to his.

The New Testament writers use almost mystical language to capture this connection: You are now "in Christ." You can no longer be separated from him. When Jesus dies, you die. When Jesus rises, you rise with him. Your new Lord cannot be held by the powers of evil and death, and therefore neither can you. As long as you remain beside him, you are safe. You are saved. You have changed residence from an empire falling to a kingdom rising. No power on earth or hell can turn you out of it. You belong to the future now. You belong to Jesus' future. You have been saved, and you will be saved all the more (future tense) when he finally ends the resistance forever and brings all creation under his rule.

On the other hand, the present tense suggests something important. You are being saved. There is something more going on here than only a past status change or a future promise. Even now something is changing. You are changing. You are becoming something, here and now, that you have never been before.

Ironically, the term *Christian* was first coined by enemies of the Jesus people. Early Christians called themselves "followers

---

1. For examples in the writings of the New Testament, see the following: past tense—Romans 8:24; Ephesians 2:5–8; present tense—Philippians 2:12; 1 Corinthians 1:18; future tense—Romans 5:9–10; 1 Corinthians 3:13–15. For a fuller exploration of the use of these three tenses in the writings of Paul, see Brenda B. Colijn, "Three Tenses of Salvation in Paul's Letters," *Ashland Theological Journal* 22 (1990): 29–41, https://biblicalstudies.org.uk/pdf/ashland_theological_journal/22-1_29.pdf.

of the Way." Salvation, as they saw it, was a way of walking in connection with Jesus, under the umbrella of Jesus' authority, that led to greater wakefulness, authenticity, wholeness, and freedom. Jesus *was* the Way, and as they followed him, they were moving down a path where all these gifts were growing.

Acknowledging Jesus as Lord is not, in the end, the price we pay for getting a rescue ticket. It is also not an obligation we owe for the gift after the fact. Allegiance to Jesus is the crucial context of the rescue. This is what it means *to be on the bus*. There's no other bus to ride. There is nowhere to be saved, except as part of Lord Jesus' kingdom, as part of the new world of justice and freedom that he brings. And there is no way to be part of that new world without pledging loyalty to the one ruling it. This is where the safety is—under Lord Jesus' mantle. For those who are living under that mantle of authority, things are already changing. The future isn't just coming; it is already here.

TRANSFORMATION

THE ART OF BUILDING

Personal transformation is not a fully voluntary project, as there is no way to opt out entirely. All of us are changing every day. We're being shaped by what we do and by the stories we take in. By the sermons we listen to or the commercials. Even when we're not paying attention. Even when we're not acting on purpose. For better or worse, each of us is already on a journey of becoming, and there's no (survivable) way off the airplane.

We tend to define our lives by the big choices at the cross-roads. This way or that way? We often tremble at the potential implications of a wrong call. Of course, it's undeniable that some roads lead to steeper climbs than others. But taking a wrong course also doesn't make things hopeless. God is as persistent as a cat scenting tuna; there is no path that God won't follow us down. It is never too late to turn. However, the best time for turning is always right now. The deeper a rut we wear in the ground repeating broken patterns, the more difficult and painful it can be to climb out of it.

Most of the time, crossroads *reveal* more than create. Most of who we become is shaped in small steps. Small adjustments over time that add up to radical change. We make true the stories we tell and act out over and over again. By the time we arrive at the crossroads, the decision is already written in the grooves of our brains.

Human formation has no microwave setting—not now and perhaps not in eternity either. Character is more of a slow-cooker exercise. Our true humanity is something we grow into day by day. Or it is something we grow away from a bit at a time.

Furthermore, transformation is not just the product of what we do but *how* we do it. Modern Westerners love to build and to produce. It's a pathology, nearing compulsion. We are driven to work ceaselessly to *make* the world we want to see. However, we may achieve all the external outcomes we desire in the world, and one rogue wave can wipe out the sandcastle we spent an entire lifetime erecting. And then where will we be?

Perhaps it's been a long time since anyone has reminded us that our most crucial life work is becoming. We can labor for change in the world, but we can neither guarantee the result nor make it last. We can seek to influence others, but we cannot force their movement. What we can do is fully cooperate in our own transformation. The lasting outcome is not what we build but *what we become while building it.* The process matters. The ultimate result that Jesus pursues in all his teachings is the transformed body of the builders. When all the castles crumble, this is the part that carries over from one age to the next.

JESUS AND THE ANTI-PITCH

An interesting thing about Jesus is how little effort he seems to make to "sell" his Way with rhetorical pitches that promise desirable outcomes. Modern advertising, by contrast, is full of such dazzling promises: Lose ten pounds and never feel hungry! Get rich while working eight hours a week! Land a ring from a good-looking doctor with five easy steps! Erase twenty years with this magical face cream!

Jesus doesn't promise health. He doesn't promise wealth. He doesn't promise popularity or picket fences. He doesn't promise safety; he doesn't even promise less suffering. At times you'd almost think he was trying to talk people *out* of following him. But for those who know how to hear it, there's a deep integrity to his anti-pitch. Jesus presents the naked truth of a world with no shortcuts. There are no quick fixes or painless roads. Anything worth having comes with a cost. Possessing something priceless will cost you everything (Matthew 13:45–46). That is Jesus' offer, take it or leave it: Everything. For the price of everything.

It's a high-stakes offer, not for the faint of heart. Jesus' Way isn't easy or painless. But that doesn't mean that it comes without gifts. Jesus doesn't promise health. But he does promise a journey toward wholeness. He doesn't promise material wealth. But he does promise care and attention, as well as companions for the journey. He doesn't promise picket fences. But he does promise a homecoming. Jesus doesn't promise short-run safety. But he does promise a long-run story where sacrifices are overwhelmed by gifts and no true good is permanently lost. Jesus doesn't promise less suffering. But he does promise suffering reclaimed and recycled by God so that it is never meaningless or without its fruit.

Along this Way, Jesus starts to relieve us of unnecessary burdens we've been hauling around all our lives. He begins to restore our perception of the possibilities in ourselves and others. He shows us how to avoid the pits that would trap us. And when we stumble into them anyway despite his warnings, he holds out a hand and pulls us free again. Along this Way we are saved a little more each day as lies and distortions fall away and false selves are peeled off.

THE HYPOCRISY CHARGE

The road between here and there, between where we are and where we're going, often feels intolerably long and complicated. Sometimes it's hard to hold hope for ourselves. Sometimes it is even harder to hold hope for other people. Hypocrisy is the most common charge leveled against Jesus followers by a world whose expectations have been disappointed one too many times. Odds are good that most of us have felt visceral disappointment in someone we regarded. Odds are even higher that we've felt it about ourselves.

In the long journey of transformation, ours and others, idealism is not our friend. Change often looks more like a spiral than a straight line, taking ground and losing it, coming back around a little farther than where we started. When the disciples asked Jesus how often to forgive the same person, Jesus' humorously specific answer—"Seventy-seven times!"

(Matthew 18:22)—gives us a sense of Jesus' own expectations regarding the transformation process. In other words, "You might as well settle in with each other because you're all going to be circling this thing for a while." Jesus, it appears, is not as easily shocked or alarmed as the rest of us.

The answer to the hypocrisy problem cannot be perfection, which is impossible. Neither can it be to lower our aspirations—Jesus proclaimed a whole new world, not an old one lightly dusted. Perhaps the place to begin is with a more honest and open disclosure of the process: "Dear world, we Christians know what we're meant to be, but we cannot see the whole way there. Please forgive us when we face-plant, trying to reach forward. We can't promise we will get it right next time either. But we can promise that we will never stop trying."

The promise carrying us along is that there is a design woven into each of us that we have barely glimpsed yet. There's a version of you, whole and free, untangled and undistorted, that was given for the sake of the world. The blueprint is held for you by the Designer. The process of development might be longer than you ever conceived. All the steps along the way might not yet be clear. But the seeds are already there, planted in the soil. God sees them, even buried deep, and knows what they will grow. God is not hurried or impatient. God is planning forever with you around. You are not yet what you can be, what you *will* be, by God's grace. But it will be—*you* will be—glorious as the full design emerges.

This is your story. It is also the story of everyone one else you know. A story worth remembering when idols fall and our heroes show their weakness. A story worth remembering when our enemies reveal their most destructive faces. A story worth remembering when we are forced to confront our own deepest shadows.

You can be patient with yourself in small beginnings and becomings. You can afford to be gentle with others too. Five or ninety-five years is nothing—we are all just getting started.

THE POWER OF PROXIMITY

Some hear the description of early Christians as "followers of the Way" and imagine this Way as a set of abstract ethical ideals. The ideals can be embraced without specific reference to Jesus himself. In this conception, "Jesus" serves primarily as a symbol or rallying point, representing the sort of idealized human life by which the world might be improved.

It is true that the salvation of Jesus can't be separated from a concrete way of living. The two are integrally related. Salvation as Jesus taught it looks less like a golden ticket and more like a golden road that, if followed, leads inexorably to life.

But we are also not in a situation where all our collective efforts at bootstrapping will get us where we need to go. We all start out trapped in quicksand, and only someone not in the quicksand can pull us out. Furthermore, the biggest obstacle to our becoming is not a lack of right ideas. Only perfect love provides the safety we need to repent and change. This condition is not something any of us are equipped to provide for each other. We must have it from our Creator if we are to have it at all.

Transformation is ultimately a function of relationship, of critical proximity. We are changed as we follow Jesus. We are changed as we apprentice him, imitate his patterns, learn from his behaviors. But more than that, we are changed *by the proximity itself.* We are changed by contact with him. We are healed by being in his presence. As we see the truth embodied in him, we become less susceptible to lies. As we experience the world through his eyes, our tastes and aesthetics change. As we are loved by him, we grow less paralyzingly afraid. As we are named by him, we finally become ourselves.

To confess Jesus as Lord is not primarily an intellectual commitment or an ethical project. It is a commitment to relational proximity, to make ourselves available to a presence that is itself the centerpiece of all human transformation. It is a commitment to follow Jesus, to be with him, to be identified with him, to function in union with him, to be marked and altered by him. Through this whole process, we are being saved—saved from fear and greed and self-deception. Saved by love and for love. Nothing else can produce the bone-deep change that we need. Nothing else makes us truly what we already are—citizens of the future, people capable of being at home in the new world that is coming.

CONVERSATION STARTERS

1. What do you think is the relationship between Jesus the Lord and Jesus the Savior? Does it matter where you start? Why or why not?
2. Why do you think early Christians chose to call themselves "followers of the Way"? How might you describe some of the contours of this Way?
3. If Jesus is the first true human, how does he challenge our ideas of what true humanness looks like?
4. How does it feel to think of putting yourself under the authority of someone else (i.e., Jesus)? Are there parts of you that resist this idea? Why?
5. Where might following Jesus as Lord take you that you wouldn't otherwise go if you were following only your own instincts or logic?

4

God's Secret

A New Role for the Collective

DILEMMA

STATUS: IT'S COMPLICATED

It's hard to find a person these days who doesn't have complicated feelings about the church. Each year a smaller percentage of Westerners affiliate with one. Each year those who do affiliate show up less often. It's not just the religiously disaffected but also devoted Jesus loyalists who are having real doubts about the place.

Each person has their own story, and their own reasons for a keeping a distance. If you believe that religion is just the "opium of the masses," perhaps a couple of hours scrolling memes in bed covers the same bases. But among those who give at least some credence to the possibility of God, there are four explanations often offered for opting out of Sunday:

Reason #1 for opting out: Church is boring and pointless. Weeks fly by, with limited openings for brunch or baseball with the kids. Besides, what churches are up to doesn't seem to have much to do with Jesus or his priorities anyway. Half are occupied with coffee bars and smoke machines, like some forty-five-year-old in leather pants trying to prove that he's still got it. The other half are nineteenth-century cultural museums, preserving the tambourine by sheer force of committee. Church is kind of cute and nostalgic when Christmas is in the air, but nobody craves a fruitcake on a sunny June morning.

Anyway, if I want to hear from a well-informed preacher, chances are I can find a better one on YouTube than at the church down the block. And listen to it on my own time, like while running at the gym. Multitasking, people! It's a virtue!

Reason #2 for opting out: The church has inserted itself as an unhelpful middleman in a relationship that should be more direct. No one needs a mediator or special room to meet up with God. In fact, all the religious hoopla often just gets in the way of real connection. I meet God better somewhere other than inside a church building. I encounter God while hiking. Or gazing at the stars. Or sitting on my porch with coffee. God feels much more present in all those places than while trying to contain my kids in a pew without resorting to duct tape and while being constantly distracted by someone's hacking cough.

Besides, at a certain point a person just grows beyond what the church can provide. Sunday school might still make sense for kids who think Joan of Arc is Noah's wife. But the rest of us have moved on to the mountains to join God for more advanced private lessons.

Reading #3 for opting out: The church is basically a cesspool of hypocrisy and corruption. Headlines teem with scandals from every wing of the Christian church—religious professionals abusing children, harassing women, or terrorizing congregants who have the nerve to ask a question. The bigger the stage, the more it seems to be about money or status or control. It's impossible to know whom to trust any more.

And that's just talking about the leaders. The people in the pews are total hypocrites as well. They use their religion like sandbags to shore up privilege and patriarchy. It would be morally questionable to even associate with this mess.

Reason #4 for opting out: Church is a good idea in theory; there's simply not a decent one around here. A communal expression of faith seems worth preserving. After all, relationships are important, and faith is easier to maintain when others help you hold it. It's just unfortunate that I live in the dead zone of good churches. That congregation was too old and small. This one had good preaching, but there wasn't enough room in worship to let the Spirit flow. That one seemed great for a while, until I saw that article the pastor reposted.

I'll go back eventually. I really will. As soon as work settles down. Definitely when the kids are back in school. Anyway, I'm sure I checked in at least once last month. Or was it the month before?

DISCLOSURE STATEMENTS

Hi. We've been conversing for a while now, but we haven't been formally introduced. My name is Meghan, and in the interest of disclosure, I believe I must now inform you that I've worked in a church for the past fifteen years.

Please don't stop reading.

Perhaps for some this fact alone may invalidate any reflections I have on the church. For what it's worth, you should know that in general, no one is more aware of the depths of the church's issues than your local, non-celebrity pastor. If one of those four descriptions touched a chord with you, I'm the last one to judge. Honestly, it's hard to dispute the truth of any of these points. I too often feel closer to God gazing at trees than listening to the bellowing of the tone-deaf guy behind me. I too sometimes question whether my work as pastor has much to do with Jesus. I too have fallen asleep during sermons (confession: sometimes even while writing my own). I too have cried hot tears of fury and pain because of treatment by Christians.

All this to say, if you'll believe me, I feel the questions too. Whatever we think of Jesus, something about his church seems tragically malformed. Maybe even unrecoverable. It's hard not to wonder if it's all unnecessary. Maybe Jesus would get along better if the church stayed out of his business.

THE SOCIAL SPLEEN

For all the internal factors driving the exodus from churches, this religious exodus is also occurring within the context of a wider cultural mass extinction event. Civic institutions of all kinds have been dying across the West for generations. Unions, clubs, leagues, neighborhood groups, and school organizations have all experienced significant decline. Indeed, for a time the church appeared to be the last cultural holdout.

Decades ago, in his landmark book *Bowling Alone*, political scientist Robert Putnam analyzed the data to conclude that the greatest culprit stealing social energy was (drum roll please): the television.[1] And this was before auto-play! But

---

1. Robert Putnam, *Bowling Alone: The Collapse and Revival of American Community* (New York: Simon and Schuster, 2000).

there are likely many other factors in the mix. We are impossibly busy, working long hours to pay high rents or because our job is closely tied to our identity. Or we're running around making sure our children taste every experience we can afford. We commute to work or work from home. We play online or in backyards surrounded by fences. We jog and shop with Bluetooth earbuds in. Many of us are highly mobile, moving in pursuit of professional advancement or lifestyle amenities.

Sociologists have also noted that when we do go out, we select for interactions with people who share our education level, economic status, and politics. Even our preferred coffee chains substantially overlap with our identity markers. In other words, our social field tends to be narrow and made up of people who think, and often look, a lot like us.

Different cultures have distinctive characteristics that set them apart. As a nation, the United States scores the highest in the world on a trait called "individualism," closely followed by Australia and much of Europe. Cultures high in individualism place a significant value on self-expression, self-reliance, individuality, and personal choice. Social norms and structures bend to support these values.

Christianity in the West has been mingling with the cultural value of individualism for centuries, with visible effects. Where it was once assumed that the community was the proper place to discern the Bible's meaning, now it is the individual who must read and determine meaning for themselves. Where being a Christian once meant belonging to a group—sometimes even a nation—now it is understood as a personal commitment that does not, and should not, require public validation. Where following Jesus was once believed to implicate large-scale social structures, now it is assumed by many to primarily entail living ethically within one's own family and private projects.

In such a cultural context, even if the church did not have such glaring problems, it would still be no wonder if many questioned its purpose. The church, like most other social institutions in the West, feels a bit like a spleen—an awkward remainder of some previous era of human evolution. If all these spleens start causing problems—as they have a way of doing—it makes sense to just cut the darn things out.

INDIVIDUALISM AND ITS SIDE EFFECTS

Individualism has now had hundreds of years to work up a good head of steam in Western cultures. More than enough time for the practical outcomes to begin to make themselves clear. Fair to say, results have been complicated.

On the one hand, greater emphasis on the individual has led to important moral breakthroughs. It has enabled wider recognition that every life has inherent worth, that every person is deserving of protection and respect. The contemporary notion of "human rights" emerges from this vital recognition. Creating more space for the uniqueness of individuals has added breadth and diversity to our collective experience of the world—in many cases both increasing enjoyment and enriching practical outcomes. Individualism in cultures has also been linked to greater creativity and innovation by encouraging individuals to find and develop their own passions and perspectives.

On the other hand, like other cultural values, individualism has often-undisclosed side effects. One side effect of individualism appears to be high rates of loneliness and anxiety. Social bonds are often weaker and social networks smaller and more fragile, easily broken when one piece falls out. Significant numbers of people report lacking any close relationship. Meanwhile, an increasing body of medical research traces the devastating health effects of human isolation; loneliness, it seems, kills as fast as cigarettes.[2] A few of the alienated act out in explosive violence that is hard to predict precisely because its symptoms fester out of view.

Another unexpected side effect of individualism has been its tendency to leave children vulnerable in particular ways. More distant community ties mean that problems like abuse can go unnoticed. Smaller social networks also result in less of a safety net for children when their primary relationships disappear or for some reason cannot provide. Even in the best circumstances, nuclear families must survive day to day with far less overall support.

Life satisfaction is difficult to objectively measure. But long-range studies suggest that relationships, not personal achievements, have by far the biggest impact on long-term happiness. Many discover this fact too late, only after decades of other pursuits fail to provide their promised fulfillment. The most common end-of-life regrets tend to relate to overwork and underinvestment in relationships.

In general, technology has enabled us to find more people like us, other pinstripe-wearing unicorn-lovers who prefer popcorn with milk. This can be truly delightful, even lifesaving in some situations. However, widespread "social selection" also comes with adverse side effects—including making others, those polka-dot-wearing unicorn-hunters, seem scarier and stranger. The more we immerse ourselves within our tailored group, the less sense we can often make of those outside of it. Vast swaths of people over there, our neighbors and fellow

2. This statistic is reported by many, including the United States Centers for Disease Control (CDC). See "Loneliness and Social Isolation Linked to Serious Health Conditions," Centers for Disease Control and Prevention, March 24, 2023, https://www.cdc.gov/aging/publications/features/lonely-older-adults.html.

citizens, feel incomprehensible, threatening, like fundamentally different breeds of human.

Questions abound. No one wants to be forced into wearing matching pajamas. But it also stinks to be alone on Christmas, or in the hospital with no one to call. Everyone wants to be understood and to feel safe to be themselves. But it's harder to understand others or to know what safety means in a world where so many feel threatened by the polka-dot people next door.

REDISCOVERY

A NEW KIND OF FAMILY

The recorded teachings of Jesus contain very few direct references to the church. Some conclude from this scarcity that the entire existence of the church must be a humanmade concept—at best a step removed from Jesus' primary project; at worst a distraction or distortion.

However, while Jesus rarely used the word for "church"—in his day a generic term that simply meant "assembly"—we have already seen that the primary subject of his discourse was a place called "the kingdom of God." As we discussed in chapter 2, a "kingdom" is not merely a personal project or habit of the heart but a collective, a social reality. The first followers of Jesus described the nature of this new collective with a variety of metaphors. *Kingdom* is a metaphor from the political world, the term for a group of people living together under a common authority. Another popular metaphor was that of a temple. By themselves, each Jesus follower was just one stone or brick. But connected like a building frame, they became a space where God could dwell. Still another metaphor was a body, in which all parts find their purpose in interconnection. When one part suffers, so do all.

But outside of kingdom, the metaphor cluster that appears most often in the teachings of Jesus comes from the family system. In Jesus' day, it was already common within Judaism to describe God as "Father." Jesus gave this metaphor special emphasis. He encouraged his followers to call God "Abba," an intimate family term much like "Dad." He compared God to a loving human parent, eager to give good gifts—and able to afford them.

One of Jesus' most beloved one-liners, often repeated at funerals, is his statement to his followers, "My father's house has many rooms; if that were not so, would I have told you that I am going there to prepare a place for you?" (John 14:2 NIV). An earlier English translation, "In my father's house are many mansions," inspired a thousand songs and fantasies of personalized castles in the sky. But what Jesus has in mind is likely not an endless row of multi-winged modern palaces. He's describing a large family home full of bedrooms, all of which share interior walls. The kind of place where if the kid next door is learning oboe, you're going to know about it.

The early Jesus followers were well known for calling each other "brother" and "sister"—a fact that generated not a few awkward neighborhood rumors when two of these "brothers" and "sisters" decided to marry each other. Yet despite ripe potential for misunderstanding, these titles were vitally important to the early Christians. They had been adopted by God. They had been made coheirs with Jesus of the future world that God had promised. This meant they were now bound to each other by a bond whose strength and permanence exceeded every other tie—including blood or marriage.

If that sounds radical now, that's nothing compared to how it rang in the first century, when blood ties and marriage alliances determined everything from your profession to your social standing. These Jesus followers were embracing a radical shift in identity, a shift that bound their reputation to someone else entirely. This new bond meant a huge, controversial change in whom they answered to, in whom they were responsible for, in whom they owed greatest loyalty.

The theme of family disruption came up regularly in Jesus' ministry. Jesus' own family relationships seem contentious at times. At one point his family attempts to stage an intervention, convinced he's lost his mind (Mark 3:21). When his mother and brothers show up at one of his engagements seeking his attention, instead of going out to meet them, Jesus shocks the crowd by gesturing to his disciples and declaring, "Whoever does the will of my Father who is in heaven is my brother, sister, and mother" (Matthew 12:50). Most perplexing of all, Jesus instructs that "whoever comes to me and doesn't hate father and mother, spouse and children, and brothers and sisters . . . cannot be my disciple" (Luke 14:26).

Jesus is speaking hyperbolically here, not advocating literal hatred. But he clearly both experiences and anticipates some level of tension between the new social order he is initiating and the old system of common loyalties. If belonging to Jesus means joining a new nation, many will find themselves living in a different country from their families of birth or even marriage—living under different laws and logic, with different customs and culture. Conflict is inevitable in such a situation.

Jesus encourages his followers, who might well feel alarmed at the conflicts and losses involved in moving into a new world, "I assure you that anyone who has left house, brothers, sisters, mother, father, children, or farms because of me and because of the good news will receive one hundred times as much now in this life—houses, brothers, sisters, mothers, children, and farms (with harassment)—and in the coming age, eternal life" (Mark 10:29–30). The timing of the promises—*now in this life*—is critical, because everyday life requires real support. It may be telling that Jesus' ministry seems to have particularly attracted single women, among the most vulnerable people in the first-century world.[3] His offer of a new structure of social connection was apparently taken seriously, both by those with everything to lose and by those with everything to gain.

GOD'S SECRET PLAN

In a letter to Jesus followers in the urban center of Ephesus, the apostle Paul claims that God has been sitting on a secret. For generations beyond number, God has been working a hidden plan behind the scenes of history—a plan that only now, in Jesus, God has decided to disclose. You have to admit, this is a pretty good setup for a viral article.

So what is it, Paul? What is this big, secret plan that God has been driving all things toward? "This plan is that the Gentiles would be coheirs and parts of the same body, and that they would share with the Jews in the promises of God in Christ Jesus through the gospel" (Ephesians 3:6).

---

3. I was first alerted to the significance of this fact in Joel B. Green, *The Gospel of Luke*, New International Commentary on the New Testament (Grand Rapids: William B. Eerdmans, 1997), 318.

The Jewish people were (and are) a family group, related by blood as well as faith. But according to Paul, God's relationship with them was the first phase of a larger plan. Since the beginning of time, God has been dreaming of building a bigger, weirder, even more unlikely family. This has been God's secret plan: to adopt some wildly diverse kids from every corner of the globe to live in glorious chaos in one massive family home and to inherit together the lavish goodness of everything that belongs to God. Thanks to Jesus' actions, the adoption has now gone through.

While modern Christians like to sing lyrics like "I am a child of God," early Christian phrasing was usually plural. First John 3:1—"See what kind of love the Father has given to us in that we should be called God's children." *We* are called God's children—love has been given to *us*. This adoption is not just about a new bond between an individual person and God. To be adopted is to be enfolded into a family system; it is to accept a place and role within an integrated household. The family isn't incidental to the adoption; it's key to the point.

God is building this family for sheer joy, but Paul suggests that God has an additional agenda: "God's purpose is now to show the rulers and powers in the heavens the many different varieties of his wisdom through the church" (Ephesians 3:10). The rulers of the world cannot unite diverse people for love or money. We've all seen this as a fact. The unseen spiritual powers working against them are far too good at tearing things apart. The only thing reliably strong enough to overcome our human divisions is a war with somebody else. World peace is pretty much a pipe dream until the aliens provide us with a common enemy from outer space.

But God is throwing down the gauntlet with the unseen rulers and powers, saying, "You big posers think you're so clever in the ways you divide. Well, get a load of my church: they belong to every culture, nation, personality, and philosophy; they don't have a blessed thing in common. But look at how I can make enemies into siblings; look at how, bound together in me, they make each other stronger."

The church is meant to school the rulers and powers in the "many varieties" of God's vastly superior wisdom. It is a boundary-crossing, stereotype-defying, awkward-embracing, interdependent, and mutually supportive family whose very existence reveals to the powers that be just how powerless they are. The church is meant to be God's holy taunt to every spiritual power or human politician who profits by stoking division: "You think you're all that because you've managed to split atoms. You can't even imagine the energy that will be emitted when I start bringing things together."[4]

HOUSEHOLD CODES

An ancient "household code" was a list of instructions that laid out roles and responsibilities. In the Greco-Roman world, such codes were directed almost exclusively toward the all-powerful male head of house. Early Jesus followers expanded and modified the genre, addressing *all* household members as persons with dignity, agency, and moral choice. Jesus himself shows no particular interest in defining specific role divisions. He does, however, speak in depth about the "rules of the house" in which God is the parent.

In God's house, Jesus makes clear, there are no primary suites. The greatest makes themselves least. Anyone who

---

4. My understanding of the church was profoundly influenced by two books in particular: (1) Philip Turner's book *Christian Ethics and the Church: Ecclesial Foundations for Moral Thought and Practice* (Grand Rapids: Baker Academic, 2015); and (2) Christena Cleveland's book *Disunity in Christ: Uncovering the Hidden Forces that Keep Us Apart* (Downers Grove: InterVarsity Press, 2013).

aspires to the privilege of leading will be the first to serve (Matthew 20:26–28). In this household, everyone will be afforded honor and respect.

In the family of God, everyone gets loved and the black sheep of the family gets loved the hardest. This is the point of Jesus' most famous parable, the prodigal son (Luke 15:11–32). Many families scapegoat or reject their problem child; God's family throws a party each time the wanderer returns.

In God's family, resources are shared wherever they're needed. Jesus identifies himself with his sick or struggling siblings: "Whatever you did for one of the least of these *brothers and sisters of mine*, you did for me," he says (Matthew 25:40 NIV, emphasis mine). That is how this family rolls. The burden of one is carried together; the gift of one is a gift to all.

In God's household, there is no quiet avoidance of speaking of problems. This household practices accountability, because family doesn't leave family stuck in a bear trap if they can help it. If you can't pull the trap off alone, Jesus says, this family calls in reinforcements (Matthew 18:15–17). This family can also, when necessary, exercise firm discipline when someone's flat refusal to stop setting bear traps in the hallway threatens them and others.

The family of God keeps no records and holds no grudges. This is perhaps its most defining feature. Jesus is clear and firm on this point: "If you forgive others their sins, your heavenly Father will also forgive you. But if you don't forgive others, neither will your Father forgive your sins" (Matthew 6:14–15). This is not a threat but a simple statement of fact: in this household, mercy is a way of life. To belong to this family is to practice forgiveness. There's no way to exempt yourself without moving yourself out of the house.

THE PLACE WHERE IT HAPPENS

Modern ways of speaking often make relationships sound like the cherry on the sundae of a fulfilled human life. Every person should be whole alone. Self-sufficient and independent. Completely self-defined. But there is a deep inhumanity to this expectation that many sense and suffer for, even if the nature of the problem is hard to articulate.

Self-care isn't enough. There are times when we need to be carried to the water that will heal us. Self-definition isn't enough. We need to be frequently reminded of the truth of who we are. Self-actualization isn't enough. We often reach our full potential only in concert with others.

The good news is that God created no only children. The church is not a building. It is not an institution. It is not a particular set of rituals or procedures. It's a shorthand name for the whole raucous household, stretched across time and space, that Jesus won—a gift for himself and a gift to each other. For better or worse, when you hook your wagon to Jesus, all his siblings come with him.

Let's be real—we all know there are reasons it can be easier alone. Alone won't hurt you. Alone won't disappoint you. Alone won't break your heart. Alone won't steal and wreck your car. Alone won't hold you back from moving for your dream job. Alone won't eat the last of the ice cream you were saving.

But God wants something better for us. Something none of us have truly had yet. Something we probably wouldn't have ever dared to dream of on our own. A real place of belonging, where we will be loved and celebrated. A place where burdens will lighten as other hands help carry them. A place where other mouths will multiply our laughter. A place where difference will evoke delight and wonder. A place where we'll become ourselves by learning what is uniquely ours to give.

A new community is both the means and goal of God's transformational activity.

We aren't there yet. God knows we aren't there yet. The communities we've encountered are all broken in so many ways. But God has been working this plan since the start of time; this isn't the year that God trades it in for an upgraded blender. The future isn't a bunch of lonely ghosts haunting private mansions. It's a family home with a huge backyard where somebody is always awake to talk to and someone is always out back tending the smoker. This is where it's going. All whom Jesus adopts get the household with him.

But here's the important thing—the perfect, idealized, Someday Family isn't just the ultimate goal of God's activity; the imperfect, non-ideal, conflict-ridden family-as-it-is is also key to God's process for getting there. It's the deeply flawed place where the change starts, where God's dream begins to become real.

Paul writes to the local church ("assembly") of Jesus followers in the city of Corinth, "You are God's temple and God's Spirit lives in you" (1 Corinthians 3:16). The *you* here is plural. God is present with individuals. But Jesus himself noted that when humans come together, even in small numbers, something different happens. God's presence becomes somehow more tangible; God's power is amplified. Where Jesus people gather, what emerges is more than the sum of the parts (Matthew 18:19–20).

This mystery of multiplication has practical consequences. For those who are gathered, personal transformation accelerates. Faith sparks faith and risk sparks risk. Wisdom grows with more eyes to notice. Bear traps are released faster. In the presence of deeply flawed and often annoying others, grace and truth and forgiveness and patience get a daily workout. We get practice in all the things that living as siblings ultimately means.

For those who haven't (yet) joined the family, there are consequences to this amplification of the power and presence of God as well. We said in chapter 2 that God's big project is redeeming all creation. In this chapter, we've exposed God's secret plan to adopt a giant family. In the next chapter, we will see these are not two separate stories but one. The secret plan is key to achieving the big project; redemption is the family business.

TRANSFORMATION

CHRISTIAN WITHOUT CHURCH

Can I be a Christian without going to church? In some eras of history, the answer has seemed obvious: "No! The church is holding heaven's keys. Cross it, and you've crossed God." In other times and places, the answer has seemed equally obvious: "Yes! God is the only one who can judge. All that matters is where you stand with Jesus."

The question turns out to be more complicated than it first appears, because so much ultimately hangs on what you mean by *church*. If church means a place with a steeple where people gather for early morning sing-alongs and juice shots, we are probably quite right to place it on the nonessentials list. The very idea of sacred buildings as the place where God dwells was fundamentally disrupted by early Christianity. Jesus himself is God's announcement that God isn't sitting in God's house, just waiting and hoping that someone will roll out of bed and knock on the door. God is taking to the streets where normal people work and live. "Get ready," Jesus says, "because God is coming where *you* are." This is what incarnation means—God coming to you; God *with* you. God's presence inhabits not buildings but human bodies.

It is, however, a quite different thing to ask, "Can I be a Christian by myself, without the necessity of doing life with those irksome other Christians?" Within the frame of Jesus' teachings, this question is a bit like asking the server, "Can you bring me a slice of apple pie, but hold the apples?" So, um, you'd like a pastry shell with a side of sugar?

The issue here is not that God will fail you for not getting out of bed or for skipping choir rehearsal. The issue is what it means to be a Christian in the first place. According to the earliest definitions, a Christian is someone who offers Jesus allegiance and in doing so becomes part of a new society. A Christian is someone who accepts God's invitation to adoption and becomes part of a wild, weird, and (sometimes) wonderful household full of siblings.

In the kingdom of God, there are no private villas. There's only the one big house. If you're God's, this motley crew is yours whether you're on speaking terms or not. You're bound to them and they to you, come heaven or high water. There's no formula for family. It isn't defined by what you do in a certain two-hour window on Sunday. Family doesn't mean, my beloved fellow introverts, that there is not ample space for silence or refreshing solitude. But if you're looking for a world without the messiness of siblings, without the necessity of loving even the ones you cannot stand, Jesus' kingdom is not the place to find it.

THE WORK OF TABLE-SETTING

Jesus' vision of a new family is challenging in several directions at once. People belonging to cultures more like Jesus' own may resonate with his experience of how new loyalties disrupt old family ties. For those who were raised in cultures high in individualism, the challenge may be almost the opposite: embracing our place in a household that necessarily includes other people. It's not just us anymore. We didn't choose these people, but nevertheless, they are ours. We are now responsible to them and for them. Our fate is bound to theirs.

Then there is the challenge that occupies many early Christian letters: learning to love people radically different from you. Getting along was hard enough when all the Christians were Jewish, sharing a common culture and a common history. Now adoptions were occurring all over the world. Diverse practices and preferences, eating habits and moral convictions, collided with each other. Offense was given, and taken. Harsh words were spoken. Feelings got hurt. Some attempted to bar others from the dinner table. Much of the writing that makes up the Christian New Testament comes from early Jesus followers grappling with the diversity of their new siblings, wondering "What on earth has Jesus *done*?"

Two thousand years later, the very questions of culture and diversity that occupied the early Christians have come alive again as the world is getting smaller. We are (slowly) learning the importance of more voices at the table. But power differentials are multileveled and complicated. And for every ten voices, there are twelve distinct opinions. Some of these differences we recognize as (passionately held) aesthetic preferences. Many others carry serious moral weight. We cannot seem to agree on the stakes of the fights or how to distinguish the categories of morality from preference, let alone agree on the desirable outcomes. How many forks does a table setting properly require, and who gets to decide?

There are no quick or easy answers for navigating diversity. But it's worth recognizing where these questions land in the scheme of the Christian story. They are not secondary concerns but cut to the very heart of God's no-longer-secret plan of forming a big, diverse family that feasts together at one table. Expanding our palette of appreciation, holding out chairs for our siblings, passing the platters of abundance— these are foundational spiritual practices. They are how God's dream comes alive.

DISILLUSIONED AND DISAPPOINTED

So where does all this leave those who are bored, disappointed, disillusioned, frustrated, or profoundly hurt by the church?

Let's be clear: God will love you even if you don't "go to church." Jesus' close friend Matthew writes of him, "He won't break a bent stalk, and he won't snuff out a smoldering wick, until he makes justice win" (Matthew 12:20). The God of Jesus is gentle with the wounded. Many people have tried to lock God inside their building or ideological system. None have ever succeeded. Jesus walks through the walls and goes on his way. He can find you where you are.

At this point in history, it would also be impossible to credibly argue that the church is not a bit of (or a lot of) a hot mess. Every local gathering of Jesus followers is made up of people much like you, with their own wounds and their own biases and their own issues they're working through. They get distracted and preoccupied with their own concerns. They frequently think they know far more than they do. They sometimes learn at the pace of an upside-down turtle. If you think your life would be easier and less painful if you just stick with Jesus and skip his posse, you'd almost certainly be right.

There's only one real argument I know of for choosing to engage: most of the things worth having we can't get alone.

We have said that Jesus comes to save us from our traps and make us into true humans, fully grown in the image of God. But no one becomes fully human alone. The image of God is relational. We discover ourselves, we are born into our humanity, in connection with others. As we are helpless and cared for. As we sacrifice for others. As we forgive and are forgiven. As we find what is uniquely ours to offer.

In his letter to the Christians in Ephesus—a letter which focuses on the church, in all its glory and struggle, the apostle Paul shares what he is praying for:

> This is why I kneel before the Father. Every ethnic group in heaven or on earth is recognized by him. I ask that he will strengthen you in your inner selves from the riches of his glory through the Spirit. I ask that Christ will live in your hearts through faith. As a result of having strong roots in love, I ask that you'll have the power to grasp love's width and length, height and depth, *together with all believers*. I ask that you'll know the love of Christ that is beyond knowledge so that you will be filled entirely with the fullness of God. (Ephesians 3:14–19, emphasis mine)

Grasping the depth of love. Being filled with all the fullness of God. It's hard to imagine better gifts to ask for. But it's easy to miss the context of Paul's prayer. Paul is praying for the church, the community, in its diversity and difference. He is praying that *through trying to live together* in this glorious mess of family, the Ephesians' capacity for love will be increased. He is praying that *through their very complicated togetherness*, they will come to discover how wide love reaches, and in doing so will become more like God.

We cannot come to know love's width and length, height and depth, alone. Alone we only know it reaches as far as us. We cannot be filled with God's fullness alone. God is love, and love is not a solo sport. We are filled with God's fullness as we work out love with others.

As we will see in the next chapter, we also have a mission, a role to play in God's rescue of creation. That mission is not effective alone. It is in a real community, practicing love across difference, even in the midst of pain and wrong, that the world will truly glimpse the power and wisdom of God.

A community doesn't have to be perfect to become part of any of this. It doesn't have to get every idea right. It doesn't have to sit in pews on Sunday mornings. It doesn't have to be certified "Free of Screwups and Hypocrites." It does have to be together, practicing love and forgiveness, suffering with and for each other across the divides that define the rest of the world. In the end, the church is not a place we go; it is a community we become when we start living out our family code and living into our family mission.

From the very beginning, to follow Jesus was to become part of his band of followers. This band included Zealots— political radicals and revolutionaries, hoping to overthrow the government by violent force. It also included tax collectors—institutionalists who personally profited from the corrupt status quo. The first time Jesus invited Matthew the tax collector over for dinner and he and Simon the Zealot locked eyes, you can only imagine that things got real awkward. Chairs set at opposite ends of the table. Jesus frogmarched into the side room: "Lord, seriously, *are you out of your mind?*"

These first followers of Jesus were initially held together by nothing but a common invitation and adoption. And yet, it was enough. They were changed by proximity to Jesus and to each other. Both their starting assumptions and philosophies were upended. Together they rethought the world and practiced being love. Jesus never imagined any other possibility. God had always planned to stake everything in creation on the massive family table.

CONVERSATION STARTERS

1. How would you answer if someone asked you, "Do I have to go to church to be a Christian?"
2. In what ways do you think the cultural value of individualism can be an asset? In what ways can it harm or limit?
3. What would you identify as some of the most distinctive practices or behaviors of God's household?
4. What does it look like right now to practice love across normal divisions? What practices or relationships would challenge you to grow in the width and length and height and depth of God's love?
5. How do we deal with our disappointment or disillusionment when the church fails to be what it is called to be?

Noah and the Crusaders

A Reimagined Vocation

DILEMMA

BUILDING AN ARK

Every year or so, some long-haired prophet assigns the world an expiration date. So far, predictions of apocalypse have been vastly overstated. In March 1988, God did not appear as promised on US television channel 18 to announce God's impending descent. In 2011, 2.8 percent of the earth's population did not abruptly vanish just before the onset of devastating earthquakes. Nor in the fall of that year did Comet Elenin end it all in a fiery collision with Earth.

Still, with democracy on a knife's edge, the planet threatening ecological collapse, and college dropouts hoping to make a quick billion reinventing Frankenstein's monster, now seems as likely a time as any for total annihilation. The End Is Nigh? Yeah, that sounds about right. So what exactly do you do for a world that seems one sneeze from disintegration?

Many generations of Christians have been formed in the Noah School of Disaster Preparedness. Perhaps you've heard the story: Ancient man learns the earth is going under, builds a gigantic boat, and fills it with all the good people he can find, plus matching sets of animals (except the T. rex who dealt in small arms and therefore couldn't be trusted). The flood breaks loose, and the good folks and their gators hunker down and wait out the global devastation.

More than a few Jesus followers through the centuries have concluded that Noah had the right approach. The church is the ark; your best bet is to tuck inside and wait until the chaos passes. The primary role of the righteous as concerns the rest of the world is simply to try to convince the neighbors to board the boat as well—either by threatening them with thumbscrews or by luring them in with a trail of bounce houses and free coffee mugs.

This school of thought remains alive in some quarters. However, it has recently gone a bit out of fashion. For many it's stomach-turning to imagine watching from a cruise ship deck while the rest of the world drowns. Most of us don't really want to be the last survivors eating freeze-dried food in the bunker while children next door starve. Not to mention the need to account for the sorts of instructions that Jesus gave his followers: "Heal the sick, raise the dead, cleanse those with skin diseases, and throw out demons" (Matthew 10:8). Driving out demons is difficult when you're sealed in a boat with only the angels.

THE NEXT CRUSADE

If Noah's approach to engaging a planet in crisis leaves you feeling a bit seasick, there are plenty of other approaches to choose from. A far more popular biblical model is the Joshua School of Global Conquest. Joshua was the military commander leading the campaign when a group of rescued slaves conquered the land of Canaan in the name of God. Sometimes the people marched and sang and prayed, and the resistance mysteriously collapsed. Sometimes they charged in with spears and arrows, stood over the corpses of their enemies, and gave all the glory to God.

During the Middle Ages, graduates of the Joshua School were often called Crusaders. Crusaders marched to foreign lands, converting residents at sword-point and claiming ground for the kingdom of God. They were promised heavenly reward for their righteous activity. Today it all sounds rather barbaric and horrifying. Few believe that the world's dire problems will be solved by sticking guns to heads and declaring, "Choose Jesus or else." But the logic of the Joshua School has proved adaptable to more "civilized" modern expressions.

The underlying logic sounds something like this: Jesus is Lord. He is the world's true ruler, the one who speaks for God. Everything would be better if everybody would do what he says . . . Therefore, it's the sacred duty of his followers to conform the world to his desires in any and every way they can. It's the mission of the church to apply every tool it can grasp to cut down the resistance, seize ground for king Jesus, and set up his kingdom for him.

Modern people tend to be more comfortable a step removed from the sword. Therefore the government itself becomes, more often than not, the tool of choice. Whoever controls the political apparatus gets to set the rules the paid swords will enforce. Where the church can rally our troops in sufficient numbers and motivation, we can take the metaphoric ground. We can glorify God by taking control of world affairs. We can actually build this kingdom we've been waiting for.

In the meantime, if people are wrong, so the Joshua logic goes, it's our righteous duty to let them know. If they won't listen, it's our duty to let them know louder. If they still won't listen, we are honor-bound to speak of nothing else.

Let's be honest—much of this logic feels compelling and intuitive. Surely a person should do all they can to further a cause they believe in. Surely they should speak for what they think is right. Yet recent history has also raised troubling questions. Is any action justified if the outcome leaves us closer to kingdom-of-God-conditions? How far can you go? Joshua slaughtered women and children to gain control of Canaan. Lying, selectively omitting, cheating, stealing, killing, "verbal slaughtering"—what, if anything, is off the table, and why? Whatever the answer, it's not so obvious that Jesus followers have reached consensus about it.

Then there are even more pragmatic considerations. It turns out that no one likes to be called names or kicked in the back of the knees. Sooner or later, people forced to bend tend to rise up and kick back. Tactics that temporarily claim a mile may end up losing ten by helping to consolidate a powerful backlash. Even supposing it does work—that it does prove possible to *make* more bodies kneel before Jesus—it's less clear whether captive citizens are the sort that Jesus Christ came seeking.

STAY-AT-HOME RELIGION

Partly in response to the ugly historical results of the church flexing its collective muscle in the public sphere, some Jesus followers have concluded that religion is best kept inside the house. Faith, they reason, is a private matter between a person and God. An individual should pray, go to church if it suits them, and try to be a good person in all spheres of existence. As concerns everyone else, it's best to stay out of their bedrooms, out of their wallets, and generally out of their business.

On the whole, the crusader approach has been more popular historically. Being action-oriented, it tends to be more fun. But the privatization of faith has a particular appeal in the present context of pluralism. In a world where everyone's beliefs and values are so different, perhaps the best we can do is shut up and keep out of each other's way. Many secretly wish the crusaders would just grab some cucumber water and chill out for a minute.

The School of Stay-at-Home Religion is the more modern cousin of the Noah School. Both share a core strategy of non-interference. As an overall approach, the School of Stay-at-Home Religion seems less arrogant, less violent, and less judgmental than its competition. The primary trouble is that, as many have noted, non-interference is often just a fancy name for complicity. The very middle-class preference for "not making trouble" has propped up many evils, including segregation and white supremacy.

In reality, many—even most—find themselves pulled back and forth between different items on this menu of responses. They reel away from colonialism, the crusader-like tactics and force-fed faith of some historical camps of Jesus people. Yet every time Joshua logic gets evicted, it seems to find a way of slipping back in through the backdoor, disguised in a spiffy modern hat. The causes deemed worth fighting for change across time and various camps, as do the allies. Harder to shake is the intuition that the best route to progress for the world is for Jesus' people (and their enlightened allies) to be driving all the cars and occupying all the palaces.

MIRROR IMAGES

We find mirrors of these same approaches in the wider world. Secular liberalism arose as society at large was being forced to grapple with increasing diversity in values and in beliefs about the answers to the world's problems. Christianity in any flavor is no longer accepted as the default. The theory of how we would operate this brave pluralistic new world was simple in its earliest iterations: we would teach that difference is good and that no one has a right to judge anybody else.

There was a moment, brief in retrospect, when this answer seemed persuasive. "Tolerance" became a core value taught to children in schools. Right and wrong were understood to be in the eye of the beholder, too culturally laden for broad public enforcement. What happened in the bedroom was no one's business but the adults inside. "Don't judge and don't be judged" appeared the peak of modern moral wisdom. You might note how similar the logic sounds to the non-interference of Stay-at-Home Religion.

However, challenges were quick to appear here, too, and were difficult to ignore. Tolerance is a wonderful idea—until you discover that other people believe some truly intolerable things. Hateful ideologies and conspiracies spread like wildfire online. Meanwhile, cultural prophets have observed how tolerance often favors the status quo and buffers those in charge. In the wake of revelations of abuse and increasing questions about how free "consent" actually is, the moral wisdom of staying out of others' bedrooms no longer seems quite so universally applicable.

These troubling realizations produce a powerful swing back toward the crusader-mindset. A new set of secular fighters have arisen to claim ground for what is right. The tools on the table take all sorts of forms—media, company policy, law, campaigns of social pressure. Just as for Christians of the Joshua School, the logic feels almost irrefutable. Should we not shout as loud as we can for what is true? Should we not use every weapon we have to slay the wrong and erect the just?

Yet as with Christian iterations, here too the real-world results are complicated. No one likes having the back of their knees kicked, regardless of who is doing the kicking or how pure their motives might be. Angry people tend to freeze in position like fast-dry cement. Self-righteousness, bitterness, and cynicism grow as resentment echoes back and forth between opposing camps. Even without religion, a culture can condemn colonialism while also reinventing it. The practical result of sincere efforts to create positive change is often just more division and hate.

There is a genuine bind here that we all can recognize. The world needs change. The status quo is deadly. Some things are truly intolerable. But a planet full of people swiping at each other's knees doesn't necessarily make things better.

REDISCOVERY

A NEW VOCATION

The early Christians firmly believed that Jesus followers have a role to play in the cosmic rescue story. But their understanding of that role bears strikingly little resemblance to Noah's ark,

Joshua's conquest, or stay-at-home religion. Their approach seems to have been derived from close study of the mission of Jesus himself.

The apostle Paul writes to the Christians in Corinth, "If anyone is in Christ, that person is part of the new creation. The old things have gone away, and look, new things have arrived!" (2 Corinthians 5:17). Some English translations of the Bible are more apt to say, "If anyone is in Christ, he (or she) is a new creation." This is a grammatical distortion, likely influenced by the Western bias toward individualism. It treats Paul's words as if his primary interest were the change occurring within the single, self-contained person.

The phrase as Paul actually writes it is broader: "When anyone belongs to Jesus . . . new creation!" Look! It's here! New creation emerging! A new world in them. A new world around them. A change in creation itself. A new way of seeing all of it, through the lens of Jesus and the self-giving love of the cross. There is certainly a personal dimension to this picture: the one who encounters Jesus and binds their life to his begins the process of becoming a citizen fit for earth-as-heaven. But this personal dimension is folded into a much larger event: a transformation taking place in the structure of reality itself.

Paul explains to the Jesus followers in Corinth that this world-change is happening because of God's direct activity and intervention in history. It is also accelerating as *they* embrace their own commission. It turns out that when they chose to follow Jesus, they not only began an apprenticeship in being truly human, but also accepted an apprenticeship for a public job.

All Jesus' apprentices are being trained for a new public position. Paul describes the job like this: "God . . . reconciled us to himself through Christ and . . . gave us the ministry of reconciliation" (2 Corinthians 5:18). It may be useful to hear the term *ministry* less in a religious sense and more in the sense in which it's used by the British Parliament. Any citizen of Jesus' new nation is immediately assigned an apprenticeship within his government's Ministry of Reconciliation.

REVERSING ENTROPY

Like *salvation*, *reconciliation* is a shorthand term used by early Christians to talk about God's project of global rescue. Everything in the cosmos seems divided, spinning rapidly apart. Modern physics has discovered that the space between each star is expanding extremely quickly. Some (very) future human could look up at night and see only empty sky. As the universe is going literally, so (metaphorically) goes the earth itself. Here, too, the space between every group and object appears to be increasing: Nations divided. Genders. Racial and ethnic cohorts. Gaps growing between political parties, between humans and animals and land. Families separated. Human beings alienated from their own bodies and minds.

God has undertaken a project of undoing separation, reversing the damage this rending has done to the cosmic fabric. God is reversing entropy. God is closing the distance. God is bringing divided people back into right relationship. God is bridging the gaps. God is saving the world. God is reconciling creation, putting all things back together.

God's Ministry of Reconciliation has many branches— "divisions," if you will. Each division plays some role in the larger mission: God is resolving our world-ripping doubts about whether we have worth. God is reconciling us to our bodies so we can live at peace within them. God is tearing down the walls that divide ethnic groups so each can guard the others' interests. God is ending the gender battles so all can use their strengths to bless. God is breaking patterns of isolation so all can experience intimacy and belonging. God is bridging the gap between rich and poor so all can live in abundance. God is healing the relationships between humans and the non-human created order so that all living things can flourish together.

All of these are extensions of God's project, branches of the Ministry. This, the early Jesus followers said, is what God is accomplishing in Jesus. God is tearing down walls and constructing bridges. Reconciliation is God's business. As it happens, God's business is also family operated. As Jesus puts it, "Happy are people who make peace, because they will be called God's children" (Matthew 5:9). All God's adopted daughters and sons have a job in some division. Peacemaking, bridge building, wall deconstruction—this is what we do. This is what it looks like to be part of the family.

MADAM AMBASSADOR

Perhaps another metaphor may help illuminate the nature of the job. Paul tries this one on for size: "[God] has trusted us with this message of reconciliation. So we are ambassadors who represent Christ. God is negotiating with you through us. We beg you as Christ's representatives, 'Be reconciled to God!'" (2 Corinthians 5:19–20). You might say that every citizen of God's new nation is assigned an ambassadorship. Each person is sent out somewhere in the world as an official Reconciliation Regime representative.

To be clear: the role of an ambassador is *not* to invade a foreign country. The American ambassador to Canada would be in a world of trouble if she stormed Ottawa and tried to seize control of all the syrup stockpiles. This act of aggression would work against the spirit of the role.

An ambassador is a representative of one country living peaceably in the midst of a different one. Ambassadors are, by definition, foreigners who do not fully belong to the place where they dwell. An ambassador's primary job is to represent the values and interests of her leader, to speak and act on her leader's behalf, expressing her leader's desires. Ambassadors make the case for all the benefits that peace with their leader can bring. "Ally with my nation," an ambassador says, "embrace its ruler and his terms, and see how we'll all flourish together."

An ambassador works from an embassy—a plot of foreign soil in the middle of another nation. Within an embassy, the laws of the ambassador's home country preside. In this place where an ambassador labors or dwells, a different culture and set of customs are exemplified. An ambassadorship is far more than speeches; it is a fully bodied, life-encompassing identity.

REDISCOVERY #5:

Jesus' people are sent as ambassadors
for God's reconciling work.

This is how the early Christians learned from Jesus to understand their identity and place in the world. They were foreigners to every place they lived. They belonged to a different nation they'd been called to represent publicly. They were being sent on an ambassador's mission of representation and appeal. It was a mission of speaking and living both. Their words announced the will of their Ruler. Their actions exemplified the values and possibilities of life within his nation.

THE BEAUTY OF OUTSIDERS

One of the favorite terms of early Christians to describe their role was *witness*. By *witness*, they didn't mean a passive bystander staring open-mouthed at a traffic accident. A witness in the original sense is someone who doesn't just watch but testifies to what they have seen. A witness can vouch for the very real existence of an alternative set of possibilities, a different way that things could be.

One of the beauties of being a foreigner, an outsider to a regime, is your ability to see through a culture's so-called inevitabilities. The lifelong residents of a nation often take their experience, good or bad, as just the way things are, the way that they *must* be. It benefits the powers that be to have them think that this is so. But the ambassador appears as a living witness to a wider world beyond. The ambassador can say with the authority of personal experience, "I come from a different place. I live under a different rule. I can tell you from my own experience—it doesn't have to be this way."

It doesn't have to be this way. We don't all have to be frantic, anxious, or perpetually angry. It doesn't have to be this way, men and women in a zero-sum game for well-being. It doesn't have to be this way, the poor afraid of starving and the rich afraid of stealing. It doesn't have to be this way, a life's worth measured by what it can produce. It doesn't have to be this way, a dinner table full of people who can hardly look at each other. It doesn't have to be this way, human beings enslaved to technology we invented to serve. It doesn't have to be this way, everyone rising and falling and living and dying alone.

Jesus deploys his followers as ambassadors, sending us to live on some plot of foreign soil. Everywhere we go, individually and together, our lives are a bold declaration to the world: It doesn't have to be this way. We are the King's appeal. We are living billboards for his offer: There is a better country. There is a better way of living, a better way of being human. There is a Lord giving away citizenship in a land of more opportunity and hope than you have ever dreamed.

LIVING FLAGS AND PUBLIC TASTINGS

The job of ambassador is categorically distinct from the default approaches to world-change that have caused so much conflict and devastation. Unlike the Noah School, there is no pattern of withdrawal. Ambassadors are sent to live outside; engagement is their job. An ambassadorship is fundamentally incarnational; it requires putting down a body where other people live. The process of appeal happens not in verbal drive-by but in long-term, embedded relationship. The appeal includes not only *claims* of another possibility but living *demonstrations* that make the claims credible.

Also unlike the approach of Stay-at-Home Religion, the role of ambassador is a public function. It requires a person to be visibly different and to have a way of speaking about why. An ambassador must be respectful of others and their values but does not claim neutrality as the ultimate good. The ambassador's job is to make the case for a specific ruler and his desires. The ambassador has a side—but that side is defined quite apart from the internal politics of where he is "stationed." His loyalty belongs to his leader and to his home country.

Unlike in the Joshua School, however, ambassadors understand from the start that their job is not to exert force or impose their will on foreign territory. An ambassador's role is primarily invitational and persuasive. The ambassador makes the case, describes the benefits and, when necessary, the potential consequences. The ambassador does not deploy his staff in the dead of night to paint stars and stripes on other peoples' doors or plant foreign flags on their lawns. But he does occupy his own assigned plot of soil as a living signpost, a living flag of sorts—a constant reminder of the existence of another country.

Jesus followers sometimes like to speak of "building" God's kingdom. Like many metaphors, this one gets very slippery. More than once, such a metaphor has inspired a battalion of eager Jesus followers to show up in hard hats on some random street, declaring, "We're building a twelve-story skyrise for Jesus here—whether you like it or not." The neighbors rebel: "Who do you people think you are? That's my home you're steamrolling!" Many things can be built this way. A reconciled new world isn't one of them.

Proper job distinctions are crucial to the early Christian vision. God is the architect. Jesus is the primary builder. Jesus' followers—we are first and foremost *the building itself* (Ephesians 2:21–22). This building can do many active, public things. It can witness to the beauty of the Architect's eye for design. It can hold public "tastings" of the Possible—tastes of a different country, tastes of a different logic, tastes of a different mercy, tastes of a different kind of life. It can host refugees who are fleeing shattered homelands in search of safety. It can speak truth to the powers. But God is the one doing the building. The kingdom is built as the rest of us start to *be* together the building we are.

THE TEAM-BASED MODEL

The operative word here is *we*. In ambassadorship, isolation does no one any favors—neither the ambassador nor the mission itself. An effective embassy includes a whole staff working in concert. Jesus himself deployed his followers in pairs (Luke 10:1). He described the way his followers (ambassadors) will carry his authority by saying, "Where two or three are gathered in my name, I'm there with them" (Matthew 18:20). Jesus is committed to a team-based model of mission.

There are many advantages to a team-based approach. In ancient Jewish tradition, a minimum of two witnesses were needed to convict a criminal, because two eyewitnesses speaking together were deemed more reliable. One speaking for a foreign king could be lying or full of delusion; many speaking together are a credible delegation. One person living differently might well be a fluke; a community living differently indicates the presence of a pattern, a common origin.

Team approaches bring together a diverse range of gifts. An eloquent speaker may be useful for an embassy's function. But just as important is someone who can run the computers and someone who can train the kids in the home country's language. Someone who keeps disease from spreading. Someone who can fix the plumbing when the toilet backs up. The mission isn't going far if nobody gets fed. If only the extroverts show up to public events, there will be no ambassador to the wallflowers, hiding out behind the curtains. Reconciliation, with its many branches and divisions, requires many kinds of workers, operating in coordination. Sometimes many different hands must chip at a wall to see that wall fall down.

A team-based model also has the benefit of decreasing the risk of rogue ambassadors. We hate to admit it, but it happens from time to time—an ambassador gets full of the glory of her title and starts drag-racing in limos, parking in no-parking zones, substituting her leader's desires for peccadillos of her own. The team is the reminder that ambassadors aren't kings, a check against rogue ambassadors who might take the embassy hostage and attempt to renovate it into their personal palace.

Most important of all, ambassadorships are not solo endeavors, because of the nature of what is on offer.

Reconciliation is about a new way of being together across previous divides. It takes two or three together to form an outpost of a different country's ways of loving, forgiving, sharing, valuing. Only a community doing life together is equipped to model what it represents. Paul says, "We are ambassadors" (2 Corinthians 5:20)—*we*, again that pesky plural. The relationships among the ambassador team are the most potent form of appeal—or anti-appeal—that an alternative kingdom can make.

TRANSFORMATION

A MISSION IN TWO PARTS

One of Jesus' first followers, a first-century tax collector named Matthew, described the way Jesus spent his time like this: "[Jesus] announced the good news of the kingdom and healed every disease and sickness among the people" (Matthew 4:23). The two verbs in this sentence—*announced* and *healed*—are category summaries not just for Jesus' own activities but for the actions of his followers after him.

Jesus did not gather followers into a stadium with a retractable roof to wait for history to end. He also didn't deploy them with weapons to storm the palaces of Pilate or Herod. Instead, he sent his followers out to do what they'd seen him do. Jesus' favorite words were "Follow me"—in other words, "Apprentice me." He instructs his disciples, "Go! . . . Whenever you enter a city and its people welcome you, eat what they set before you. Heal the sick who are there, and say to them, 'God's kingdom has come upon you'" (Luke 10:3a, 8–9).

Notice the distinct echo of Jesus' own activities—something to say, and something to do.

Heal the sick. Healing comes in many shapes and sizes. Every form is an expression of God's reconciling power, God's ability and intent to put divided things together. Jesus told his followers to offer tastes of God's reconciling power, tastes of what God wills to do. No purity test is required to earn these demonstrations. They are to be offered as free gifts. The love of God, after all, is always there, long before any human deserving. These demonstrations are key to the credibility of the message—"Here is the mercy that exists, that is already reaching toward you."

Say to them, "God's kingdom has come upon you." In a first-century Jewish context, the implications of physical healing extended beyond the body. Healing involved a removal of social stigma and shame, a restoration to community. The healing offered by Jesus' followers is meant to be a signpost pointing to something even bigger. Healing is an indicator of a God present and active in the world. Healing is the revelation of a Ruler who cares, who is working to put all things back together. It's not just a random, lucky occurrence or an achievement of human cleverness. It's a gesture of love and a letter of divine appeal, an invitation to embrace a more comprehensive and permanent rescue.

Jesus also gave instructions on what his followers should do where their ministry of reconciliation was not welcome. Not everyone, it seems, will be ready for such wholeness. In such cases, Jesus' disciples were to respect the boundary lines drawn from the opposite side. They were to simply shake the dust off their feet and move on, trusting the result to God (Luke 10:10–11). Their job was to make the offer, not to secure the outcome at any cost or refuse to take no for an answer.

It's hard to imagine a simpler or more practical model for collective ambassadorship. There is power deployed toward healing. Any and every kind of healing. Offered irrespective of person or possibility of payment. And there is the verbal task of helping healing be understood in a larger context. There is no invasion. Or you might more properly say, this is what God's kingdom looks like *when* it invades a foreign land. It announces its arrival in a relentless volley of healing and deliverance. The only force that can stand against it is the human refusal of consent.

THE WOUNDS OF WAR

In Paul's description of ambassadorship, he sums up the ambassador's appeal by saying, "We beg you as Christ's representatives, 'Be reconciled to God!'" (2 Corinthians 5:20). For some this language—"reconciled to God"—has become a major stumbling block.

Some groups of Jesus followers have taken this phrase to mean that the only way for Christians to help the world is through evangelism. All the world's problems will be solved by persuading more people to be followers of Jesus. There is little use in doing work without a conversionary focus and little reason to cooperate with those who are not Christians.

Other groups of Jesus followers are tempted to dispense with the "God" part of the equation. Evangelism seems arrogant and oppressive; even speaking about God in the modern world feels like a distasteful imposition. Might as well just get on with the work of making the world better. Help people heal and groups reconcile—no need to bring God into it.

Both approaches fail to see the integrated nature of the whole picture. Paul's point in speaking about reconciliation with God was not that Christians can do no good without first converting someone. Sometimes people encounter Jesus and then discover new possibilities for reconciled living. Sometimes people experience reconciliation and in doing so meet the One who makes it possible.

The first centuries of the church were filled with the latter kind of stories. Healing miracles—God's reconciling power at work to restore health to bodies—are one common example from the first century. But there were many other kinds as well. Jesus followers engaged in deliverance work—helping free people who suffered from the oppression of evil. Even as an obscure minority group, Jesus followers became known across the early Roman Empire for all the poor they cared for and hungry they fed. In times of plague, Christians were noted for caring for the sick, even at great risk to themselves. In these works of justice and mercy, healing and deliverance, people saw glimpses of a gracious God they had not known. Many became believers in Jesus. The reconciling work was the kingdom's first and most powerful herald.

At the same time, the early Jesus followers understood that lasting reconciliation of any kind was not possible without God's involvement. God's power is the fuel that healing runs on (more on this in the next chapter). Working reconciliation without Jesus was like building Disneyland's Main Street. The exterior form may look convincing. But there's not enough underlying structure for the town to be inhabited for long. The appearance of peace lasts only as long as a sword can enforce it. Or as long as a strong, charismatic leader holds the walls up from behind. The minute the sword is lifted or the leader lets go, everything often falls apart.

The early Christians were neither naïve nor especially optimistic. They understood that some forces powerfully repel each other. In their judgment, there was only one force in the universe strong enough to hold natural enemies together: Jesus himself. The force that Jesus exerts is *attractional*. It is not a kick from behind. As people are drawn by him, attracted and attached to him, they come back into proximity and proper relationship with each other. "He existed before all things, and all things are held together in him," the early church said (Colossians 1:17). This was the bottom line. Between healing and announcing, there is no "proper sequence"—God's opening moves are flexible. But pursuing reconciliation without God at the center is like trying to construct a solar system with no sun.

The indispensable role of Jesus followers in the world is to treat the disease, not just the symptoms. To be clear—we should still treat symptoms. We should patch all the wounds we can manage. This is a God-given work of mercy. No act of love is wasted. But the trouble is, for every wound we wrap, evil makes two more. Fortunately, Christianity has more to offer than bandages in the middle of battle. Because there is One on the field with the power to change the tide of the war itself.

Jesus can change hearts and undo fear-distortion. He can deliver from the corruption of greed. He can heal the soul wounds that keep people enslaved to destructive powers. He can break the grip of evil that is fueling cosmic chaos. The work of binding wounds, of healing broken bodies and broken systems, is vital work. But it is work done in the context of a God determined to stop the war.

"Jesus is Lord," the early church proclaimed—this is the only reason anyone should feel safe to lay down their weapons. Jesus followers are peace-wagers, sent to combatants on all sides of the field to say, "There's a reason to put up your weapons. There is Someone offering amnesty and calling for allegiance. He has a more excellent way than this one that leaves you both wounder and wounded."

FINDING YOUR APPOINTMENT

The church is an embassy. We are meant to be visible. Audible. God's public notice sign, the announcement of a new construction project. The church is meant to be a preview of coming attractions. Our life together is a taste of the future, Tomorrowland, existing in the present. We are Jesus' appeal to all neighborhoods and nations of what he can do where he is given willing charge.

Each individual Jesus follower has some role to play within this larger story. Ambassadorships under this regime are not reserved for religious professionals. You are never too young to be named an ambassador. Nor is this a role from which you ever retire. If you have offered allegiance to Jesus, you have been given a lifelong assignment. Your job is to fully inhabit some piece of soil, representing the values and possibilities of a restored world. Your life and words present God's appeal, "It doesn't have to be this way!" You have been authorized by King Jesus to offer citizenship on his behalf.

Some people worry about how to find their divinely designated piece of soil. Wherever you are is a good place to start. You are ambassador to that office. To the hospital. To the nursing home. To the park. To the school. To the basketball court. If you are currently there, assume you already have an opening assignment.

So here you are, Ambassador. Where on this ground are there people divided? From each other? From their bodies? From creation? Where is the system curving away from God's dreams of just peace? Wherever the gaps are, you have an opening. A place to make your body a bridge. A place to walk through walls. A place to witness to the existence of an alternative possibility. A place to call in the reconciling presence of God.

When you see a gap, approach it respectfully and prayer-fully. You don't have to think you have the answers or the power to save anybody. Better for everyone if that delusion has already died. God has the power and the answers. Your role is to approach curiously and humbly, looking for opportunities to participate in whatever God is already doing to nudge things toward each other.

And remember to seek partners everywhere you can. It's not all on you. It can't be. A prayer labyrinth is a path that looks a little like a maze except there are no dead ends or false turns. An outdoor labyrinth is often made of lines of small guiding stones. If you stay between the guiding lines of stones, turning back and forth, eventually you wind up directly at the center—the very heart of God. Notice: One stone, sitting in a field alone, does not point anywhere. An isolated stone is not a path. But when many small stones play their assigned role, side by side with others, a sense of direction emerges. A path someone could follow toward God.

COMMISSIONING

An ambassadorship begins with a commissioning. Stand, if you wish, to receive your commissioning, and answer:

Do you recognize Jesus as the true Lord of heaven and earth?

Do you promise your loyalty to him and to the laws and values of his nation?

Do you accept his commission to be an ambassador of his beauty, justice, and goodness?

Do you dedicate the ground where you live, play, work, and rest as an embassy?

Will you help take down walls wherever you find them?

Will you make your body a bridge on which others can cross to meet each other?

Will you announce with your words and life, "It doesn't have to be this way"?

Will you tell others there's a place and purpose for them in God's new world?

If so, in Jesus' name, we recognize you as an ambassador of the future. Be bold, courageous, and creative. Scatter invitations wildly. This kingdom's borders are open and the land is spacious. The king is calling, "Come!"

CONVERSATION STARTERS

1. How do you see the Noah School, Joshua School, or Stay-at-Home Religion playing out within Christianity? What are the strengths and weakness of each approach to the world?
2. What do you think is the relationship between reconciliation to God and the many other kinds of reconciliation the world needs? Can one be effective without the other?
3. What would it look like for you personally to function as an ambassador? What is your current assignment? Where are your openings to tell other people, "It doesn't have to be this way"?
4. Where does the world most need the church to model and witness to an alternative possibility?
5. What is the distinction between treating symptoms and causes? Do you think this distinction is meaningful? Explain.

6

Broken Bootstraps

A Rediscovered Presence

DILEMMA

THE PLAUSIBILITY PROBLEM

It might seem we could end things here. If what we've said so far was the common story that Jesus people were telling, it would be a vast improvement over the disembodied, God-dreading, world-despising stories that many of us have encountered in the past. But we're not done yet. Because while these five "rediscoveries" answer a set of dilemmas in both church and culture, behind each one a significant problem still lurks. Perhaps you've felt the lingering tension.

Chapter 1: We made the case for interpreting Scripture through the lens of Jesus. Jesus is the authoritative arbiter of conflicting claims of God's desires. But the question remains:

Which Jesus, exactly, are we talking about? We've all seen his many portraits. One Jesus sports a whip and a cut of abs that would make Captain America blush. Another is ethereal and dreamy-eyed and looks like he has never seen the sun. It's one thing to claim that we should take our divine disputes to Jesus. It's quite another to recognize Jesus when he shows up.

Chapter 2: We saw that God is on a mission to rescue all creation. Salvation is God's action to end evil's occupation and to "heaven" all of earth. But how exactly will this rescue be pulled off? There's a popular saying: "God has no hands or feet but ours." Forgive the frankness, friends, but if that's the case, the world is in big trouble. Some of us have a child attached to each leg and hands currently juggling a work computer, mop, dog dewormer, and a plate of Tater Tots. Just surviving through lunch is a challenge. Being asked to don a cape at eleven at night to go out to save the city will likely just result in us sleepwalking off some roof.

Chapter 3: We suggested that being Christian means coming under new authority. Belonging to Jesus includes commitment to follow his counterintuitive way in every part of life. The trouble is, Jesus' first-century words often seem rather distant from twenty-first-century questions. The subject index of Jesus' recorded teachings doesn't include climate change, dating apps, social media fights, birth defects or genetic selection, radical life-extension, factory farming, or nuclear war. Even if you want to follow Jesus, it is hard to do so if you can't tell what direction he's going.

Chapter 4: We argued that there are no solo Christians. A big, diverse family is God's greatest dream, and God's chosen way of working. It sounds so good on paper—everybody wants world-class relationships. The problem is actual people. They don't conform to fantasy. Many are difficult. Most are regularly annoying. Some seem downright unlovable. The ideal of relationship always vastly outpaces our actual experience. We regularly get the hots for some community's profile picture and show up to the date only to discover the thing was photoshopped.

Chapter 5: We learned we have a role to play in God's global rescue mission. We have been commissioned as ambassadors of reconciliation to offer tastes of a different world. The challenge: When it comes down to it, most of us don't have a clue what we're doing. We don't even know where to start. Being told to go "reconcile the world" is like being asked to reconstruct an unread book from a dump truck of confetti. Our hair is regularly set on fire by our own family members; it's hard to imagine how we'd help warring nations get along.

On paper, the Jesus story sounds compelling, maybe even (dare to hope) somewhat persuasive. But put down the book and spend a few hours in the real world, and it's suddenly hard to remember why any of it seemed remotely plausible.

BEAUTIFUL STORIES

Jesus people aren't the only ones to struggle with a gap between theory and practice. Many groups, religious and otherwise, tell a beautiful story about what could be. This is exactly the energy that fuels most political and social movements: the promise of a better world. Activists, politicians, professors, preachers, talk show hosts, even advertisers—they're all storytellers, seeking to capture attention (and votes, or money) with a vision of Hope and Possibility.

Most of us are so used to being sold something, we've gotten a bit jaded. But from time to time, someone comes along who slips beneath our defenses. A cultural prophet, young

politician, or eloquent religious teacher captures our imagination. Their story taps an unarticulated longing. The messenger
seems authentic. We want to believe it could all be true. We
toss up an online post declaring our support and sign on with
the movement.

But the promised revolution rarely materializes. The community doesn't live up to the glory of its story. Christianity, of
course, is one such movement that has left many once-believers
painfully disappointed. Even more people feel this way about
their political leaders. They rallied, voted, and donated on the
hope of something different. But nothing ever changes.

The Western world is increasingly post-religious. "Post-
religion" itself is a movement, evangelized with promises of
goods to be unleashed: Liberty! Enlightenment! Happiness!
But it's debatable whether even post-religion can deliver on its
hype. We may turn out to be intellectually freer yet also mysteriously more anxious and depressed. Societally we may be
liberated from confining stories of the past, but at the cost of
our ability to believe any story at all. Every voice that claims to
speak for truth seems to have an agenda. Cynicism and skepticism color the world gray. It's not clear why anyone should
take one story of reality over any other. The post-religious revolution has come, but it's not obvious that humanity is better
off. We may have merely chosen a different set of problems.

It's not just the movements that have failed us. When we're
totally honest, we might admit we are even failing ourselves.
A chasm exists between our stated ideals and our daily living.
The self-help industry grows every year, but our bootstraps
are broken. No quantity of books or coaching does the trick.
Most of us can't even buy the books that we write ourselves.

ETHICAL JESUS

A portion of Western Christianity is trying to correct the errors of the recent past: Christianity has been closed-minded, unwilling to learn or listen. Christianity has been judgmental, prone to legalism and moral hysteria. Christianity has been ignorant, refusing to take science seriously. Christianity has been prudish, denigrating the body. Christianity has been arrogant, failing to acknowledge mystery and forcing a vast universe into toddler shorts.

In an effort to rectify these mistakes, some reframe the Jesus movement ethically. Jesus is a moral system, the spread-sheet title for an advanced set of values and norms. Teacher Jesus instructs humanity on how to be more loving, more just, less exclusionary. Whether or not the Jesus story is historically true, they will say, it's worth repeating because it inspires higher ideals. The church is worth keeping around because it provides a useful corrective to individualism—and also because some of us enjoy a good potluck. There is a way of reading the first five chapters of this book that could come off rather like this—a version of the Jesus story that constructs a frame of logic for being better people and doing better things for the world.

In a post-religious context, this version of contemporary Christianity has its merits. It's humbler than versions that assert exclusive possession of certain truth and assume that anyone who disagrees is ignorant or evil. It's more palatable to nonreligious neighbors, who typically have plenty of room for nice people with noble ideals. It's also practical, offering con-crete instruction and wisdom tested by time. You don't have to be religious to see the benefit of sabbath as an antidote to the modern productivity addiction.

The major downside (if you see it that way) to this ver-sion of the Jesus story is there's nothing particularly unique or transformative about it. Nothing sets it qualitatively apart from any other human-invented philosophy. This is, in fact, what many ultimately conclude—Christianity is one way of trying to be good, nothing more and nothing less.

This version of the Jesus story can tell us what is good to do for the world. But it has little effect on our capacity to enact those things. Nor does it materially affect our desire to do so. It can persuade us that a purchase is worth making but puts no resources in our bank account. It can instruct us what direction to drive but offers no roadside assistance when we get stuck nose-down in a ditch.

Here again is where I step from behind the literary curtain and put my own cards on the table: if all that the Jesus story involved were chapters 1–5, I would probably not be a follower of Jesus. Not because I don't think it would be nice if everyone believed in a kinder God or tried to live up to heavenly ideals. But because I'm not persuaded that Ethical Jesus has power to change much of anything.

I've been a human for a while now. I've met others of my species. Many of us believe a lot of different things, often quite passionately. And regardless of our philosophies or our level of conviction about them, living is hard for all of us. Changing is even more difficult. No amount of diet apps and motivational speeches typically gets us over the hump. We are creatures with a special gift for falling in love with things that hurt us. On Monday we swear "allegiance unto death" in a fit of principled passion, and by Thursday all we can think about is why oh why does the stupid toaster work so slow.

I would not personally be a Christian for rediscoveries #1–5 alone. But I am one. Why? Thank you, friend, for asking. I am a Jesus follower because there is more to his story than this. If you've been around Jesus people for a while and it isn't obvious what's missing, this itself is a sign of how far the story has drifted from its earliest telling. Rediscoveries #6 and #7 concern the power that fuels the rescue mission, that makes this whole story more than a daydream.

REDISCOVERY

PHASE TWO

Jesus' public ministry lasted around three years. That's less time than it takes most students to get an undergraduate degree. The more you think about it, the wilder it seems. The guy sent to reveal God and revolutionize the world had roughly thirty-six months to get it done. Many leaders can't force a desk chair through the bureaucratic tape in that amount of time.

Jesus gave some speeches announcing that God was up to something. He healed and fed some people, all within a geographical area smaller than New Jersey. After a while, some stories went viral, and a few dozen followers grew to thousands. Energy sizzled. The smell of revolution wafted through the air. People who'd been disappointed many times before thought, "This feels different. This time things might actually change."

Then Jesus gets arrested. Within hours, he is dead. Block letters appear on the darkened screen: GAME OVER. His apprentices were barely C students. Jesus hadn't had time to build a movement that could outlast its founder. With his death, the whole thing sank faster than a bag of bowling balls.

Then Jesus appears again. After his funeral. His followers are gobsmacked but obviously thrilled. Half the city watched him die, and now here he is. But before anyone can work out exactly how to dump this barrel of lighter fluid on the movement's embers, Jesus announces that he doesn't intend to resume his old job. He's not even sticking around.

According to Jesus, he's completed phase one of God's cosmic rescue plan. Now phase two is about to begin. But phase two has a different captain. Someone else is coming to take the baton and carry the movement forward. Jesus is clear: The phase two Captain is working in lockstep with him. They are partners, sharing one plan and one project manager. She will pick up the story he started and carry it forward in the same direction.[1]

THE PHASE TWO CAPTAIN

Jesus describes the situation like this:

> But now I go away to the one who sent me. None of you ask me, "Where are you going?" Yet because I have said these things to you, you are filled with sorrow. I assure you that it is better for you that I go away. If I don't go away, the Companion won't come to you. But if I go, I will send him to you. (John 16:5–7)

Jesus here nicknames the phase two Captain "the Companion." Elsewhere the Companion is given another name: the Holy Spirit. Jesus claims it is better to have the phase two Captain than it is for him to stick around. His apprentices,

---

1. In my writing, I sometimes use male pronouns in reference to God. In this section on the Holy Spirit, I've chosen to include female pronouns. The grammatical gender of the word for "Spirit" is feminine in Hebrew (the language of most of the Old Testament) and neutral in Greek (the language of the New), which in my judgment makes it a ready place to gently stretch our imaginations toward a fuller picture of the God in whose image both men and women are made.

one might imagine, are skeptical. After all, who can carry on a movement better than its founder?

Here's the thing they haven't figured out yet: In this man who stands before them with nail holes in his hands, God is present to the world in a single human body. But Jesus of Nazareth, the first-century Palestinian, can be physically present in only one place at a time. The phase two Captain is not so contained. The Spirit is God's presence *dispersed*. Through the Spirit, God plans to be present to Planet Earth in millions of bodies and communities at once.

The plan was not for God in Jesus to work three years, then take early retirement and leave his followers on their own to finish global renovations. God had initiated this project in sending Jesus, and God planned to personally see it through. But the moment after Easter represents a major transitionary phase in God's restoration project.

An often overlooked aspect of Jesus' story is *how* he preached the sermons and performed the miracles for which he is famous. Perhaps it seems too obvious for comment—Jesus is God; he was born with magic in him. But this is not at all how the early Christians saw Jesus. In becoming human, Jesus emptied himself of all his divine powers (Philippians 2:6–7). He didn't show up with a few neat tricks hidden in his back pocket in case of emergencies. He entered the world a naked, vulnerable human like the rest. Jesus' power to heal, to deliver, to see what was hidden, had to come from somewhere else.

At the start of Jesus' ministry, before he preaches a sermon or performs a miracle, Jesus is baptized. At that moment, his friends later record, "Jesus saw heaven splitting open and the Spirit, like a dove, coming down on him" (Mark 1:10). The Spirit's presence in the world often looks much like the wind—rarely directly visible, but revealed by what it moves.

This divine Wind, this divine Companion, holds heaven open wherever Jesus goes after this. The Spirit is the power source that fuels Jesus' human ministry. Jesus only ever acts in Spirit-partnership. Throughout his years of ministry, before Jesus heals or delivers or makes major decisions, he goes away to pray. It might seem strange that God incarnate *needs* to pray. What is he doing anyway, talking to himself? Jesus explains, "I can't do anything by myself" (John 5:30). With every natural human limitation, he must listen to the Spirit articulating God's desires. He must ground himself in the Spirit's power, which equips him to respond.

The Spirit, who appears visibly at Jesus' baptism and powers his subsequent ministry, is the very same Companion he later promises to his followers. When Jesus returns to heaven, he says, he will send his Companion to be theirs. This Companion knows God's mind and has access to God's resources. The Spirit will join them on Jesus' behalf as partner in change and in mission.

REDISCOVERY #6:

The Spirit guides and resources God's mission.

One day not long after his resurrection, Jesus disappears. His followers are more than a little concerned about what they will do without him. But a few days later, on a holiday called Pentecost, the Spirit comes down, just as at Jesus' baptism. The book of Acts tells the story of what results. When the Spirit arrives with a sound like rushing wind, Jesus' followers, ordinary fishermen and tax collectors, abruptly pick up where he left off. They repeat what they heard him disclose about God. They do what they saw him doing. Lo and behold, the same sorts of miracles and transformations that happened around Jesus start happening around them.

Rome had tried to snuff out one upstart "Christ"—an ancient Jewish title meaning "anointed one," or as we might put it, "God's chosen troublemaker." The result was the multiplication of hundreds, then thousands, then billions of Christ-ians—"troublemaker minis." Never let it be said that God doesn't have a sense of humor.

THE SPIRIT OF PROPHECY

The night before his death, Jesus says to his closest followers: "I have much more to say to you, but you can't handle it now" (John 16:12). The Teacher is about to depart, and his students have been so doggone slow on the uptake they haven't gotten through half the curriculum. This doesn't appear to bode well for the future of the movement.

Jesus, however, appears unconcerned. That's okay, he says. "When the Spirit of Truth comes, he will guide you in all truth. He won't speak on his own, but will say whatever he hears and will proclaim to you what is to come. He will glorify me, because he will take what is mine and proclaim it to you" (John 16:13–14).

Jesus isn't panicked that his followers are a bit dense or that he hasn't gotten through all the lesson plans. Because he is sending someone fully qualified to keep on instructing. The Spirit will speak, like Jesus, *with* Jesus, on behalf of God.

One role of the Spirit will be to remind them of everything that Jesus has already said (John 14:26). The Spirit Instructor excels at recaps. The Spirit will bring back memory of the lessons as they're needed on the ground. She will tap people on the shoulders and say, "Remember when Jesus told you . . ." She will help distinguish true representatives of Jesus from false imposters.

But the Spirit is not just some undergrad teaching assistant; the Spirit is a fully qualified instructor, authorized to keep on teaching (John 14:26). Her lessons will never contradict Jesus; she builds only on the foundation he laid (1 Corinthians 3:11). But God is not done talking; Jesus was only getting started. There's so much yet to say.

Jesus says the Spirit "will proclaim to you what is to come" (John 16:13). She will speak about the future, about questions and situations that a bunch of first-century fishermen hadn't conceived of yet. The Spirit's job going forward will be to guide them in all truth. She will take what Jesus revealed about the will of God and bring it home to contexts half a world away and to questions no one had asked before.

As project manager for God's global rescue mission, the Spirit also often coordinates assignments. Many such stories are recorded in the book of Acts. The Spirit tells a Jesus follower named Philip to be on a particular road at a certain time (Acts 8:26–40). There, Philip strikes up a conversation with an Ethiopian traveler who eventually carries the news about Jesus to North Africa. The Spirit sends Ananias to a house on Straight Street to meet an infamous villain named Saul who is having a faith crisis (Acts 9:1–22). Saul, later known as Paul, eventually carries the story of Jesus across the Roman world.

In such cases, the Spirit provides specific guidance that allows Jesus followers to act in alignment with what God is preparing to do. Sometimes the goal is to coordinate human-to-human connections. Other times the goal is understanding itself, a tutorial in divine intent that hadn't been grasped before. This is what occurred when the disciple Peter entered the home of a Roman soldier (see Acts 10). The Spirit had told this soldier to seek out Peter, going so far as to name the specific bed-and-breakfast where he was staying. Meanwhile, the Spirit informed Peter that visitors were coming before the doorbell even rang. The meeting was so miraculous and clearly Spirit-initiated, it provided powerful evidence for a part of God's plan that the church had not yet grasped: God was extending kingdom invitations to those outside former boundaries.

Today, the term *prophecy* is often associated with predictions of the future. In the early church, it did sometimes include that, as when the Spirit warned the church that famine was coming to Judea, giving them time to prepare emergency aid. But in a larger sense, prophecy is guidance from the Spirit that facilitates the mission of God. It is one of God's core gifts to the kingdom embassies. The Spirit reveals what God is doing and what God has planned so that ambassadors of Jesus can cooperate.

THE SPIRIT OF WISDOM

The Spirit, however, is not only a talker; the Spirit is a doer. Paul writes, "We haven't received the world's spirit but God's Spirit so that we can know the things given to us by God. . . . We have the mind of Christ" (1 Corinthians 2:12, 16). According to Paul, the Spirit isn't just providing select information or an occasional cue when someone forgets their next line. The Spirit transforms minds and imaginations from the inside out. The Spirit works within human bodies to reshape neural pathways to resemble Jesus', so that over time Jesus' followers begin to reason like him, dream like him, imagine like him, think and feel as he does about the world.

Early Christians describe the Spirit as a farmer: "The fruit of the Spirit is love, joy, peace, patience, kindness, goodness, faithfulness, gentleness, and self-control" (Galatians 5:22–23). Contrary to common impression, Paul has not here composed a to-do list of virtues for Jesus followers: "Welp, time to conjure up some self-control today—one more TV episode before bed, maybe four tops." The agent of production here—the farmer of virtue, if you will—is not us but God. Paul offers a description of how a person living in sustained contact with the Companion can be recognized. The Spirit's invisible inward work will eventually show up outwardly in a character growing to look more and more like Jesus' own.

There's no suggestion that anyone generates joy or peace by gritting their teeth and trying harder. This transformation comes as a gift. The gift can be received or denied by human activity; it can be resisted or cooperated with. But it can't be produced. It must be *received* in relational proximity with One who has the power and know-how to grow it. The Spirit's work within us produces the thing we cannot produce in ourselves—an actual change in our taste buds, a change in our base desires.

THE SPIRIT OF POWER

Knowledge of what God is up to seems like a good thing. Even better if we have the desire to cooperate. But as some of us discover painfully the first time we strap on a snowboard, knowledge of a mountain and desire to conquer it does not guarantee the capacity to accomplish this aim. A rocket scientist might build a shuttle to Mars, but it won't fly far if only prune juice is feeding the engine.

The apostle Paul describes his philosophy of mission as a Jesus follower like this: "My message and my preaching weren't presented with convincing wise words but with a demonstration of the Spirit and of power. I did this so that your faith might not depend on the wisdom of people but on the power of God" (1 Corinthians 2:4–5). The early church did not believe in conversion-by-rhetoric, as if they could simply "talk people into" finding the story of a resurrected criminal credible. Jesus himself didn't choose such a strategy. He backed up his grand claims about God's goodness and God's nearness with demonstrations of power-directed-toward-goodness that got people's attention and gave his claims weight.

Jesus tells his followers, "I assure you that the Father will give you whatever you ask in my name. Up to now, you have asked nothing in my name. Ask and you will receive so that your joy will be complete" (John 16:23–24). Jesus' offer here isn't free access to heaven's all-you-can-eat candy buffet. He gives his offer crucial context by saying, "You didn't choose me, but I chose you and appointed you so that you could go and produce fruit and so that your fruit could last. As a result, whatever you ask the Father in my name, he will give you" (John 15:16). In other words, every assignment that heaven gives will be backed by heaven's resources. If the Spirit says, "Take this rocket to Mars, and tell those little green guys that God's crazy about them," the Spirit will also furnish the fuel for the ship.

God's ambassadors are neither called nor sent as rhetorical specialists. The world already has millions of people who can sell a great-sounding line; it doesn't need Jesus or his ambassadors for that. The church is meant to be the place where God's transforming presence and power are accessible. A place where people experience the new possibilities unleashed by heaven's opening. Embassies of Jesus are designed like solar thermal power plants, shaped to collect and distribute enormous quantities of change-fueling energy.

The early church talked about "spiritual gifts" as different forms of specialized empowerment given to particular ambassadors of Jesus to carry out their assigned piece of the mission. These "specializations" work best not in isolation but in coordination with each other. However, no one is ever limited to their specialty, either. Where God's Spirit goes, she does not go in parts; she brings her full self, with all heaven's goods. Every possibility, every potential, travels with her everywhere.

Ask, Jesus says, and God will give you what is needed for this moment, for this plot of ground to produce fruit. Jesus' followers have not just been entrusted with his mission; their names have been put on his bank accounts.

TRANSFORMATION

BUILDING CONTAINERS

The biblical patriarch Jacob once fell asleep in the middle of a desert, choosing a random rock as a pillow, and dreamed about a staircase. It extended from the place where he lay straight up into heaven. Angelic traffic moved up and down on it between heaven and earth. Jacob woke up and said to himself, "Holy smokes! I just stumbled onto heaven's entrance out here in the middle of nowhere! I mean seriously, what are the odds?" (my paraphrase of Genesis 28:17).

Christianity at its core is not a philosophy or an ethical system. It doesn't exist to preserve the story of a God who once a long time ago threw down a ladder to earth and might someday, if we're lucky, do so again. Christianity exists because

Jesus reveals what Jacob never dreamed: a God who has torn the whole floor out of heaven. Heavenly stairways are common as rocks around this crazy planet. *Any* place can be the place where heaven touches down.

Thanks to Jesus, the floodgates of heaven have been thrown open. The future is leaking into the present. When heaven starts leaking, there is only one sensible response: gather every container you can get your hands on to collect the liquid diamonds.

God is not waiting at a distance, disgusted or alarmed, for humans to pull ourselves together. By the Spirit, God is acting on God's own initiative in the world. God is speaking. Seeking. Nudging. Uncovering. Healing. Disrupting. With or without human help or credit, thank you very much. All those stairways will get plenty of traffic even if the rest of us are too distracted playing games on our phones to notice the angels passing through the ceiling of our kitchens.

However. For those who are awake, aware, and ready, there is a chance to get in on the action. There are ways to set out containers that allow us to gather more of the gifts that God is sending. To receive them for ourselves. To deliver them to others on God's behalf.

There is a set of habits that Jesus' people have been engaging for millennia, sometimes called spiritual practices. Prayer—a two-way conversation with God, speaking and listening for direction. Sabbath—a rhythm of God-tended rest that deliberately interrupts our frantic self-reliance. Fasting— temporarily giving up something outward to expand our inward space. Scripture reading—the potter's wheel where, turn by turn, the Spirit re-forms our imaginations for new, God-shaped possibilities.

These practices are containers. They open time and internal space for receiving. They are receptacles in which it is possible to gather the Spirit's living words, the Spirit's transforming presence, the Spirit's healing power. They are some of the key places where heaven's abundance passes into human hands, freely given to be freely dispensed.

The practice of building containers, of holding them open beneath heaven's leaking, is not an alternative to the work of reconciliation. Instead, these practices are where the fuel of the future is harvested. It is here we receive the love we will have to give. It is here we are changed into people resistant to evil's co-option. It is here we're directed to show up where God is ready to act. It is here we gather the resources necessary to share in Jesus' mission. It is here we are becoming people who can be trusted with heaven's treasure.

In the ancient story of the exodus, the Israelites wandering the desert needed fresh manna from God each day to survive. As with manna, so with God's voice. New and living words from God are needed each day for people to stay fully alive. Fresh fuel is required for embassies to keep on running. Even Jesus took regular time away from the activity of mission to build containers and gather up all that God was sending. Heaven is leaking, but you often won't know it until you put out pans to catch what falls.

CLEARING OBSTRUCTIONS

The word *repentance* gets a bad rap these days. To many people, it smacks of unproductive religious guilt, of sitting around feeling terrible about yourself. But repentance is more like an act of road-clearing. It's a term for the regular maintenance required to keep heaven's stairways open and not blocked by dirty laundry.

Jesus promised his followers the Spirit as an ever-present Companion, who would be with them individually and with their communities together. The Spirit would come and hold open a channel between the earth and God. That channel would be open wherever the people of Jesus went. Our very broken, limited bodies, and our equally limited and broken communities, can be sites where heaven touches earth. They can be places where God's power, grace, and goodness are made available to the world. Through the Spirit, Jesus opens a channel of connection that starts at our bodies and ends at the throne of God. Love, grace, healing power, divine wisdom—all of these can pass through the channel. The lives of Jesus followers can be springs from which life-giving water pours into the world.

When we fail to see the promised presence, the promised power, the promised fruit, it can be perplexing. Some start to doubt that Jesus meant his offer. In reality, many things can go wrong with the channel. Some aren't even aware it exists. God can send package after package, but they stack up unopened by the door when someone doesn't know to look for them. Sometimes the problem is that we haven't built containers to catch and hold what is flowing. God's gifts run like water straight through our hands.

But sometimes the problem is with the channel itself—the channel gets obstructed. There are things on our end of the channel that can block, distract, or sidetrack the free movement of God. Fear and self-preservation. Ego and hunger for power. Addiction, deception, prejudice, unforgiveness, and the like. All of these can clog or kink the channel so that where God sends a flood, we receive only a trickle.

The water the world needs doesn't come from us. The power to heal, transform, and rescue doesn't come from our own resources. If the channel of connection is broken or plugged up or neglected, the spring often dries up and the fruit shrivels shortly after. Repentance is the practice of clearing the channel, of straightening its bends.

There is no magic formula for receiving the Spirit's insights or power. No magic is required. Jesus says that the Holy Spirit is available for the asking, the gift God always desires to give to absolutely everyone (Luke 11:13). But there's a reason why Jesus' cousin John, before Jesus began his ministry, traveled around saying, "Someone is on his way with power to baptize you with the Spirit. So now, repent! Make his paths straight!" (see Matthew 3:2–3, 11). The open question isn't God's desire or intent to approach us; the open question is often the state of our inward roads.

This isn't a one-time project. Good roads have to be regularly maintained. Potholes form and must be filled. Sometimes life drops a refrigerator in the center lane of the highway that has to be removed. The work of keeping the way within us clear for Jesus is constantly ongoing.

SPIRIT-STORIES

With a neglect of the Holy Spirit, the Jesus movement is a car without gas. No excellent intentions, no worthy ideals, no critical project can compensate. The future cannot run on the fuel of the present. A heaven-sized mission demands heaven's power. It will drive on nothing else.

At the end of the day, I am not a Christian primarily because I believe reconciliation is a good idea. Many non-Christians think that too. I am not a Christian primarily because I believe community is a good idea. To be honest, depending on the day, I'm not always that convinced. I'm not a Christian primarily because I believe Jesus is a great and wise person. I do believe that, but the distant echo of a person two thousand years in the past is not enough for me to build a life around. I am a Christian because Jesus made extraordinary claims—about God's goodness, God's nearness, God's care, God's daily involvement in the world, and about his own identity as the one revealing these things. And I have seen enough to convince me that Jesus knew what he was talking about.

Everyone's encounters with the Spirit are different, but here are just a few examples of how I have experienced the Spirit of Jesus at work:

1. One night I attended a concert with friends. The host took up donations to help cover the band's expenses. As the donation bag was passed, I prepared to throw in the nine dollars in my wallet. Then a thought came from nowhere, "You should keep one dollar back." This seemed like such a senseless thing to do, so I threw all the cash in the donation bag. The impulse hit again, so strong that I reached inside and pulled a dollar back out. Then I felt stupid and put the dollar back in. Then I pulled it out again. The people beside me started looking at me funny as I continued fishing in the donation bag, so I threw the dollar in one final time and finally surrendered it.

Less than three minutes later a man stepped onstage and said, "One of the musicians onstage has a very sick child and the medical bills are high. I feel like the Spirit is inviting each person here to share one dollar as a special gift to help his family." Guess who, having ignored the Spirit's nudge, had no dollars left to share. Many years later, I still think about it—what it means to have a God who cares enough about the world to bother including me in a single-dollar act of love.

2. I was obeying an assignment I believed I'd been given by God, and I felt utterly abandoned and isolated. One night I hit rock bottom, crying out to God in anger and despair, "You

were the one who said to ask for what I need. Well, I need to know that you see me, that I'm not in this alone!" The next day I was in my office when a stranger knocked on the door. He was in town on vacation, he told me, from fifteen hundred miles away. Every morning he prayed and asked the Spirit whether there was something useful he could do that day. That morning, he said, the Spirit had told him to knock on this particular door because someone inside needed encouragement. I remember this man's visit whenever I begin to doubt that my prayers are heard.

3. I was walking through a shopping center parking lot to my car when I felt a strange prompting to turn around and go in the opposite direction. After about five minutes of walking away from my car, I suddenly heard someone call my name. A group of acquaintances were sitting on a restaurant patio. One said, "It's so funny! We were just talking about Jesus, wondering who could answer our questions about him, and we thought about you, and then we looked up and you were walking right past!" Following that small prompting, I was there to share about Jesus at the very moment this group of people were eager to learn.

4. I had been betrayed by a close friend. I was so angry and hurt, I could barely speak in her presence. One night I was wrestling with my resentment in prayer, begging for God's help to forgive. In the middle of the prayer, I felt something break within me, like a dam collapsing. The betrayal was swamped by the most intense love I'd ever felt for another human being. I was flooded with desire to see this person blessed, to myself be the one to bless her. What I could not change within myself in months of effort and struggle was changed in an instant with the Spirit's transforming touch.

There is a Companion who goes where no one else can. There is a voice that speaks life out of nothing. There is a presence that brings transforming energy to everything it touches. This is the new reality that Jesus won for us. Not just rhetoric or lovely stories, but power. Divine power. Unleashed upon the world to make it well, to make it whole, to make it free. God is only getting started. Heaven is open. The future is leaking. There's no greater joy, my friends, than to throw back your head and catch the rain.

CONVERSATION STARTERS

1. What is missing from the Jesus story without the Spirit?

2. Why do you think this portion of the Jesus story has been left out or overlooked for so much of Christian history?

3. Where or how have you personally seen evidence of the Spirit's activity?

4. Do you think "containers" are required to receive God's gifts? Why or why not?

5. In what ways can things within us obstruct the Spirit's movement? What other kinds of obstructions might there be?

7

The Enemy among Us

A New Perspective on Power

DILEMMA

COMPLICATIONS OF POWER

Power comes in many forms. There's the physical power to flip a mattress without getting pinned beneath it. There's the rhetorical power of TV hosts to persuade us to believe their interpretation of events. There's the social power by which freshmen have been convinced to spend a day with a live frog in their pants. There's the institutional power to shape structures to our preferences. There's the spiritual power by which Jesus and his followers mediate healing. Then there's the most mysterious and elusive form of power—the willpower to eat only one strip of bacon.

Simply put, power is the ability to get something done (or not done, as with the bacon). Without power there would be no lights, no songs, no society. Nothing would live or move or grow or change. But power is also complicated. Some of us have always been well aware of this fact. Others are gradually awakening to this reality amid a wider cultural reckoning with the shadow side of power.

Power is complicated because human interests often conflict. There are things we want or need for ourselves, for our family, for our nation. There are things we desire altruistically, for the good of humanity. But sometimes different people want things that are mutually exclusive. For example, one wants the freedom to speak his mind while others want freedom from hearing his mind spoken. Sometimes multiple parties want the same thing, and there isn't enough to go around. For example, one region's water use may leave less for those downstream. Sometimes our core ambitions for humanity conflict, as when whole cultures passionately disagree about what human flourishing requires.

Conflicting interests are typically mediated through the application of power. Individuals and groups use the various forms of power at their disposal to try to tip the world to their own benefit or toward their sense of the highest good. Even absent any malice, the exercise is fraught and messy. We may recognize another's interests as legitimate but still find them to be in tension with our own legitimate desires. And sometimes we believe that another's pursuits are simply flat-out wrong. The result is a world full of tug-of-war matches, with people pulling with all their strength in every direction at once.

To make the scene even more complicated, it turns out that power is not evenly distributed. Gender. Race. Education. Family. Intelligence. Height. Access. Money. Information. How good you look in a suit. All these factors not only affect the distribution of power, but affect it differently in different times and places. Few of these attributes are acquired by pure merit. It's like a twelve-ton gorilla just sometimes shows up for no reason and starts pulling one end of the tug-of-war rope.

Even when we try our best to level the field or set up a fair fight, it's usually impossible to hold a perfect balance for long. The gorilla often has a mind of its own. We can call in more gorillas to act as counterweights on the other side, but the result is rarely stable parity; it's usually just more jerking back and forth while the bodies pile up.

All this can be true when intentions are generally good. But power also has a way of going straight to heads and turning intentions sour. From time to time, communities get fed up with the big-headed powers that be and wrest control away from them to give to someone more worthy. But far too often for comfort or coincidence, today's revolutionaries become tomorrow's dictators. As with J. R. R. Tolkien's famous "one ring to rule them all," the hazards of power seem to increase with exposure. No one is immune. Once you learn what it feels like to have a twelve-ton gorilla do your bidding, apparently all bets are off.

CHRISTIAN HISTORY AND POWER

Christianity has its own complicated history with power.

In the early church, the power equation was simple: Jesus followers didn't have any. At least, not of the political or cultural variety. The early Jesus movement was tiny, a few thousand people within a vast global empire that was anything but a democracy.

With no power and no allies, early Christians were easy targets, regularly harassed for their various forms of "strangeness." When the emperor required political distraction, they served as convenient scapegoats. The first Jesus followers experienced bouts of intense persecution. Some lost their livelihoods. Some were exiled from their homes. Some were fed to lions in front of jeering crowds of their neighbors.

Yet strangely enough, during this period of costly power-lessness, Christianity grew rapidly. The Christian community became known for its care of the poor and its courageous martyrs. This proved a potent combination. Seemingly against every natural interest or incentive, more and more people chose Jesus.

Eventually, a critical mass was reached; there were finally enough Christians in high places to stop the killing and harassment. Christianity was legally protected. Great news! Then in very short order, the most powerful man in the empire began to call himself a Christian. Now Christianity wasn't just legal but favored, giving even more reasons to convert.

By four hundred years after Jesus, the situation of Christianity had changed radically. There were enough Jesus followers to start reshaping the Roman Empire's laws and structures, to remake the world into something more like what Christians thought it should be. This critical transition marked the beginning of Christendom. "Christendom" is a situation where Christians dominate all levels of government and culture. For almost sixteen hundred years, Christians controlled nearly every lever of power in the West—social, political, institutional, financial, military, cultural.

This might seem like an obvious good—at least to people who consider themselves Christians. After all, if Jesus followers have all the power, they can make the world more like God wants. But the record of history tells a very different story.

Christians did some good things with their power—developed hospitals, built universities and schools, started movements to care for the poor and to recognize human rights. But Christians also went on crusades, killing and pillaging in God's name. Groups of Christians tortured and murdered each other for disagreeing on the finer points of Christian theology. Christian missionaries took the story of Jesus to far corners of the globe. But they also worked to stamp out native languages and helped exploit their hosts' resources. Christian activists worked to abolish the slave trade. But Christians were also largely the ones who fought to preserve it. Recent years have added new revelations of widespread clerical abuse and institutional cover-up.

For sixteen hundred years, Christianity has held most forms of power in the West. Not only has the result not been the kingdom of heaven on earth, but to many people, Christianity appears like just another tyrant that must be tipped for humans to flourish—or even just to live in safety. It seems clear that at some point, the Jesus train jumped the tracks. What is less clear is when, and why.

LOSING POWER

Christendom is currently sunsetting in the West with a speed that has shocked and alarmed many Jesus followers. Just a generation or two ago, Christian faith seemed as inevitable as Times New Roman—the generally accepted social norm in many communities. Sincere or otherwise, minimum lip service was expected, especially by those who aspired to public positions of authority. Then suddenly . . . it wasn't. Christianity's influence over many social and political structures is steadily, rapidly diminishing. Hyperbolic claims of religious persecution are often overstated. But it's certainly true that Christian beliefs and ethics are far less dominant and even in some cases (for good reason or not) quite unpopular.

It's a hard place to be. No one likes to be the punch line of a joke. No one wants to see their movement associated with its worst examples. No one likes to feel vulnerable or out of step or to consider that they might suffer for sincerely held convictions. Most of all, no one who believes they've encountered something true and genuinely good for the world wants to see that truth and goodness dismissed.

To many it feels like the kingdom of Jesus is losing ground that it once held. Suddenly the people of Jesus have real enemies—family and neighbors tugging on the opposite side of the kingdom rope, contending for contrary ends. Many wonder how on earth they are supposed to accomplish God's desires with less and less power and more and more direct opposition.

One common response to the perceived loss of power is to seek new allies. Some do this by adjusting their Christian beliefs to be closer to the cultural mainstream. We can still get stuff done, they say, as long as we stick to things that lots of people can agree on. Others form alliances of convenience with other parties holding power. It doesn't matter whether our allies truly share our goals, they say, as long as the practical incentives are sufficiently aligned for them to accomplish what we want.

To some, history seems very much like a raw power competition. Whoever grabs the most gets their own way; the rest suffer under them. This is the base-level logic that governs most of our interactions. The United States versus China. Men versus women. Political progressive versus political conservative. Science versus religion. Humanity versus robot. Only one can win, and woe to the loser.

If this is truly history's story, the only sensible response is to grab all the power we can in whatever form we can. Our personal safety hangs on it. But more importantly, we may think, this is the only way God's mission will get done. When Jesus' kingdom is losing ground, nothing could be more cowardly than for his people to throw out lawn chairs and sip mocktails in the trenches. When the war for the world comes to your doorstep, there's no option but to stand up and fight.

REDISCOVERY

POWER UNDER OCCUPATION

Jesus himself was very aware of the consequences of power abuse. He was a first-century Jew living under Roman occupation. Rome maintained control of its distant territories through its willingness to exercise utter brutality. A fortress called the Antonia, built directly next to the temple, let Roman soldiers spy over the walls. Rebels were crucified by the highways, sometimes hundreds at a time—their slow and agonizing deaths a terrifying public warning to anyone even dreaming of defiance. Then there were the much-resented Roman taxes, payments for the privilege of remaining occupied. Jesus' own birth was haunted by the decision of a regional Rome-appointee named Herod to slaughter a couple of dozen children on the rumor that one of them might someday want his job.

By the time Jesus arrived on the scene, there was a growing Jewish resistance movement. Various revolutionary leaders had stirred small, local rebellions that ended in terrible mass executions. Yet frustration and anger continued to boil. Among Jesus' inner circle of twelve was at least one known Zealot, a member of a faction prepared to use their swords to drive Rome off, as well as a tax collector padding his pockets by filling Rome's coffers.

It's in this context of occupation, oppression, rebellion, and compromise that Jesus issues one of his most surprising teachings:

> You have heard that it was said, *An eye for an eye and a tooth for a tooth*. But I say to you that you must not oppose those who want to hurt you. If people slap you on your right cheek, you must turn the left cheek to them as well. When they wish to haul you to court and take your shirt, let them have your coat too. When they force you to go one mile, go with them two. (Matthew 5:38–41)

Imagine: one of Jesus' followers is on his way to an important dinner with Jesus when a Roman soldier snatches him off the street and forces him to haul equipment to the far side of the city. The disciple arrives an hour late to the event, red-faced with humiliation and fury. "Maybe Simon is right," he fumes, "and it's time to make heads roll."

Jesus listens to the conversation fly between twelve angry young men and then finally says, "Romans oppress Jews, Jews attack Romans, Romans crucify Jews, Jews attack Romans again. It goes on and on. Here's what I'm telling you to do instead: the next time a soldier grabs you and forces you to carry his pack for a mile, look him in the eye and decline to put it down until you've gone twice as far."

Then and now, most assume that Jesus could not possibly mean this literally. To behave this way is practically an invitation to be trod upon. But Jesus is not making doormats. Jesus is plotting revolution. He is proposing a radical strategy for shifting the battle by bringing a whole new form of power onto the field.

By Roman law, a soldier could force a civilian to carry his pack for one mile. Then he had to let the person go on their way. Imagine the soldier in the first mile, secure in his control of the situation, self-satisfied with his power and his superior position. But then his temporary hostage refuses to put the pack down. "No, no," he says, "let me take this another mile for you. I insist." What's a soldier supposed to do, wrestle for his pack? The first mile this disciple was a hostage. That second mile—probably a very quiet, awkward mile—he's something else entirely. Who is uncomfortable now? Who's in control? Who is holding the power? It's suddenly very unclear.

Rome has the power of law. The power of violence. The power of coercion. But Jesus has just put another power into play. The power of integrity. The power of generosity. The power of one's own undiminished, undiminishable humanity. The humiliation is refused, returned to sender unopened. A forced gesture is transmogrified into an unexpected gift. Evil claims the first mile but is exposed by the second, its pettiness paraded through the streets for the world to see.

REIMAGINING POWER

Jesus talks about power throughout his ministry, but the subject comes to the fore in the last week of his life, when the stakes are highest. On Sunday, Jesus is welcomed to the capital city with the symbolism and fanfare of an inauguration parade. The people throng the capital streets and make clear their intent to declare him king. They are utterly convinced he's the one sent by God to lead the overthrow of Rome. All he has to do is issue the call and rally the troops to him. They stay up late every night that week, polishing their swords.

Meanwhile, Jesus looks around at the city, then calls his apprentices together for a meal. He insists on personally washing the dirt off their feet before dinner—a disgusting job in an era of open sewage, reserved for women or low-ranking servants. He wipes the filth on a towel he has tied around his body. He breaks a loaf and talks about allowing himself to be broken for them. Then he decides on this, his final night, to give one final sermon. The topic of this last lecture: the nature of power in a world under God.

Jesus informs his apprentices they are destined for greatness: "I confer royal power on you," he says, "just as my Father granted royal power to me. Thus you will eat and drink at my table in my kingdom, and you will sit on thrones overseeing the twelve tribes of Israel" (Luke 22:29–30). Jesus appears to be giving away positions in his new cabinet. The disciples are dreaming of golden chairs and five-star dining, of servants shining their sandals and soldiers obeying their commands.

Except. Jesus informs them that power in his regime will not look like what they're thinking. He draws a stark contrast between power as humans define it and power practiced by God. "The kings of Gentiles rule over their subjects," Jesus says (Luke 22:25). Here is the most basic definition of power as human beings understand it: power is a thing you have *over* others, a form of force exerted to bend others to your will. Jesus goes on: "Those in authority over them are called 'friends of the people.'" "Friends of the people" is a term from the ancient benefactor system, where the rich and powerful do favors for the poor and powerless in exchange for more power and honor. Power under the normal human definition is an elaborate system of exchanges where those on top give to get something in return.

But, Jesus says, "that's not the way it will be with you." Hold on to your seats, disciples. Jesus is about to upend every intuition of how power operates: "Instead, the greatest among you must become like the person of lower status and the leader like a servant. So which one is greater, the one who is seated at the table or the one who serves the table? Isn't it the one who is seated at the table? But I am among you as one who serves" (Luke 22:26–27).

God's definition of power turns inside out all the normal definitions. To humans, Jesus says, the power that counts is power over others. But God's power operates from beneath them, like a servant. To humans, power functions as a system of tit-for-tat exchanges. To God, power is measured by what you give away without thanks or expectation or return.

God-styled power is exercised in doing the work that is hardest, messiest, most unappreciated. Power is kneeling before others to help them rise up whole. Power is picking up your enemy's tab. Power is bearing on yourself other peoples' dirt and shame so they don't have to wear it on themselves. Power is breaking your life open like bread so others can be nourished. God-styled power, as Jesus models it on this last night of his life, summons, invites, provokes, and serves whoever shows up at the table—friend and foe alike. It even accepts and absorbs the dreadful cost of somebody's decision to throw the gift away.

"I have given you an example," Jesus says. "Just as I have done, you also must do" (John 13:15).

Welcome to God's royal court. Do you still want those thrones, dear disciples?

THE BOOKENDS

The subject of power bookends Jesus' ministry on both sides. The significance of the beginning isn't clear until the end. At the opening of Jesus' public ministry, he is driven into the desert to be tempted by Satan. There is no leadership, no power, without profound temptation. But what could possibly tempt the Son of God?

Satan, the embodiment of evil, shows Jesus all the kingdoms of the world and says, "I'll give you all these if you bow
down and worship me" (Matthew 4:9). Seriously, man? This
is your play? You really think Jesus Christ will become a devil
worshiper if you dangle a treat in front of his nose? The true
nature of the test, the real depth of the temptation, doesn't
become clear until the last night of Jesus' life. In the middle of
the dinnertime conversation about divine and human notions
of power, Jesus abruptly says, "Simon, Simon, look! Satan has
asserted the right to sift you all like wheat" (Luke 22:31).

The same Satan who dangled power over the nations in
front of Jesus years ago has come back to play again. This
time he's not just here to screw with Jesus; he's come for his
followers too. This night, Jesus and his disciples will face the
same temptation. Only one will emerge faithful.

Jesus tries to warn his disciples—things are about to get
real, and more costly than they have imagined. Thus far, so
long as they've been with Jesus, everything has been coming
up palm branches. But it will no longer be so. "Take a bag and
buy a sword," Jesus says. The disciples are delighted. This is
the moment they've been waiting for. They tried to call down
lightning on their enemies before, and Jesus stayed their hand.
Now it seems he's finally done holding back. They whip weapons out from where they've been hiding them under the table
and say, "Great news, Jesus! We've got some swords right
here!" Imagine their confusion when Jesus says with exaspera-
tion, "Enough of that, you guys!" (see Luke 22:38).

Jesus has been trying for years to redefine power for his
followers. He's disarmed them dozens of times in a dozen different ways: "Turn the other cheek." "Give away your cloak."
"Go the second mile." "Bless those who curse you." "Pray for
those you persecute you." "No, guys, you definitely don't have

permission to call fire on cities that reject us." But still, after all this, the disciples cannot distinguish a sword-shaped metaphor from an actual call to violence. Their understanding of power still owes much more to Satan's logic than it does to God's.

They go out to the garden, where Jesus tells his disciples to stay awake and pray so they won't fall into temptation. The temptation that Jesus is worried about is the same one that has plagued him for years. This night, it returns so strong and persuasive, Jesus sweats blood resisting: "Come on, Jesus, you have armies of angels, not to mention thousands of devoted fans with swords at their disposal. Think of all the good you could do for your people, think of what you could do for the world, if you take the fight to Rome and drive those bad boys out. We all know you would be a better ruler than Caesar. Don't you owe it to yourself, to *them*, to seize control?"

Jesus wants it so bad he can taste it. Oh the good, oh the peace, oh the justice he longs to bring. He's dreamed it all his life, the deep, aching dreams of God. There's just one problem, and Jesus knows it.

"Worship me and rule the nations," the evil one had said. It turns out that this temptation was never about singing Satan lovely songs. To worship Satan is to take up his methods, take up his weapons. To worship Satan is to offer allegiance by bowing to his power-logic—to seize, to coerce, to wield power over, to rule from above. It would all be done, of course, in the name of good—of Jesus' just rule, of God's kingdom come to earth. But Jesus alone among his human siblings sees the subtle lie concealed beneath so much truth: God's kingdom built on Satan's power will not be God's at all. This, this is Satan's great Trojan horse.

Jesus cracks the horse open. He submits himself, not just to God's kingdom *ends* but to God's *means* of getting them done.

He submits himself to God's counterintuitive notion of power beneath. Jesus submits himself to the power of suffering love and to the power of broken bread and to the power of willing self-sacrifice. Having surrendered, he rises from his knees.

His disciples, who slept through the battle that decided the fate of the world, wake up and come out swinging. One of them whips out a sword and manages to hack off an enemy's ear to get the party started (perhaps wishing his apprenticeship with Jesus had come with a bit less prayer time and a bit more weapons training). But Jesus cries, "Stop! No more of this!" And he heals the severed ear (Luke 22:51).

The real significance of the moment is clear to his followers only in retrospect. "No more of this!" had been an encompassing, permanent command. There would be no more using Satan's means to achieve God's kingdom ends. From here on out, the only power in play for Jesus' followers will be God's power, the shape of which Jesus is about to definitively demonstrate.

"All who want to come after me must say no to themselves, take up their cross, and follow me," Jesus had said (Matthew 16:24). This and this alone is the form of power that evil has no shield against.

GOD AND EVIL

Jesus had announced the inbreaking of a new world under God. It all comes down to a single question: By what power will this new world be inaugurated? The power that will birth this new reality turns out to be shaped like a cross.

REDISCOVERY #7:

Evil is overcome by the power of sacrificial love.

The necessity of such a particular power, such a peculiar weapon, owes something to the nature of God and something to the nature of evil.

From the first day of his ministry to his last, Jesus was remarkably consistent in his witness to the character of God. God is an indiscriminate lover, even of God's enemies. God causes sun to shine on the evil as well as on the good. God sends rain on the righteous and unrighteous alike (Matthew 5:43–48).

Since the beginning of time, humans have stuck persistently to the intuition that divine favor falls upon the good. After all, what other incentive would we have to mind our manners? But Jesus insists that God blesses those who curse. God befriends sinners and screwups. God runs toward those who've squandered God's last dollar. God loves those who've trampled God's broken bread. God would rather die than lose a single death row inmate.

There is no way to draw near to God without embracing the great scandal at the center of God's heart: God's unreasonable fixation on rescuing everyone. Even our enemies are prized, beloved, counted among those for whom Jesus trades his own life. Paul writes to the early church, suffering at the hands of their neighbors, "We aren't fighting against human enemies but against rulers, authorities, forces of cosmic darkness, and spiritual powers of evil in the heavens" (Ephesians 6:12). Humans can be taken captive, deceived, and corrupted. Human beings can get played. But God is fighting to redeem every one of them. To be on God's side is do likewise, to recognize no person as dispensable, as disposable, as an acceptable loss.

In a war against spiritual powers, fighting evil with evil's weapons is a losing strategy one hundred percent of the time.

God's kingdom can't be built using Satan's sword; this sword will always turn backward and cut the one holding it. Even when you win, you lose. Because the kingdom of heaven is a matter not just of ends but of the means used to achieve them. It is a Way, not just a Result. Take the wrong road, and you will always end up at a different destination.

The only way to defeat an enemy is to find their place of weakness. Jesus reveals the precise location of evil's soft dragon underbelly. The only form of power that evil is powerless against is the power of self-giving love. It's a blast of light into the shadows. There's nowhere for the darkness to flee; it is done for in the moment of exposure.

When Jesus traded the sword for the cross, evil did a victory dance. Satan thought he'd won. He never imagined that Jesus' final breath, willingly surrendered for love of a hostile planet, would be the one to shatter hell and break the gates of heaven open.

TRANSFORMATION

TACTICS OF WAR

Jesus' disciples didn't understand a single bit of this when he went to the cross. First, they came out swinging. When that approach was ruled out, they went into hiding. Jesus' death seemed like the ultimate humiliating defeat. Until three days later, when the power of self-giving love proved too great for death to withstand. Only when they saw Jesus standing on the outside of his tomb did his followers finally get it. They went back over three years of classroom notes and realized: The cross was neither a fluke nor simply a one-time event. It was a revelation of divine strategy. It was a revelation of the kind of power by which God was saving the world.

We have noted that in its early centuries, the Christian church had virtually no political or cultural influence. As far as the world was concerned, they were a tiny, odd, powerless minority. Yet it was during this period that Jesus faith expanded rapidly. It took ground not through conquest or control or power over but through the application of a different set of tools.

One form of power practiced by the early church was the power of bold prayer. The first Christians understood the nature of their enemy. Their real fight was not with Caesar or his armies. It wasn't with their neighbors who mocked and despised them. Their fight was with "principalities and powers" operating beneath the surface of history (Ephesians 6:12). These were the spiritual forces fanning lies, propagating division, holding imaginations captive. This was the unseen energy turning crowds into mobs and hostages into killers and corrupting systems to their roots.

To the early Jesus followers, prayer was not passive. It was an exercise in taking the battle to the plain on which it would be decided. It was an active intervention in the fate of the world. Prayer was an act of consent to God's operation. It invited a different form of power onto the field. Prayer pushed back against the shroud of lies that blinded the nations. Prayer held ground for grace and truth. Prayer opened prison cells that would otherwise stay locked. Prayer cast out evil that would otherwise remain unmoved.

When Jesus followers prayed together, the book of Acts records, the ground itself was known to shake (Acts 4:31).

The church's prayers unleashed divine energy with power to reshape the earth. This is exactly what Jesus had promised was possible with the Spirit's coming. The channel between heaven and earth was open. Through its prayers, the early church welcomed heaven's touchdown. Heaven landed with a force that earth felt to its bones.

THE OTHER SWORD

The second form of power that Jesus followers embraced was the power of courageous witness. After Jesus' resurrection, Jesus' follower John has a vision of Jesus standing in the presence of God. The heavenly Jesus, now revealed in unmistakable glory and power, carries a sword with him. But the great surprise is where and how Jesus holds his weapon. Jesus' sword is not in his hand, where humans hold their swords; his sword is in his mouth (Revelation 1:16).

The weapon by which Jesus overcomes all evil is his truthful word. This was the game-changing insight of the early church. The world was created with a speech-act (Genesis 1)—it will be healed in the same way. The word of God, the truth of God, was sharper than a sword. It cut to the hearts of people. It sliced through the chains of lies that kept them captive to destruction. It pierced the veil of shadows.

The early Christians took seriously what they learned from Jesus at his trial. Jesus did not feel compelled to spend his breath answering every false accusation against him (Mark 15:3–5). Under pressure, he simply stood in the utter truth of every word he'd spoken and in the integrity of his life. For his followers likewise, power was found in the reliability of their truthful witness and in the integrity of lives that made these words credible.

Truthfulness and integrity didn't always protect Jesus' followers, any more than they protected Jesus. Many died as martyrs. Yet through this courageous witness, many others came to Jesus. Every blow that evil struck, every loss it inflicted, rebounded against it. Every spot of ground where martyrs' blood was spilled in faithful witness, God's kingdom claimed and owned.

This second form of power, courageous witness, was directly linked in early Christian teaching with the third and ultimate form of power embraced by Jesus' followers: the power of self-giving, sacrificial love. Jesus had said, "All who want to come after me must say no to themselves, take up their cross daily, and follow me. All who want to save their lives will lose them. But all who lose their lives because of me will save them" (Luke 9:23–24). When they were baptized, early Christians left behind their swords. Not because they were giving up the battle for the world. But because they now understood the real nature of the fight.

The first Jesus followers relinquished old, corrupted notions of power. And they gave themselves over to a new understanding of power, reimagined by God and revealed by Jesus. They were now the community of the cross. The community of power under. The community that loves relentlessly—even their enemies, even their occupiers. They were the company of those called to give their lives away for the flourishing of others. Sometimes this was a gift given all at once, in the martyr's death. But often it was a gift given ounce by ounce, penny by penny, day by day.

HEAVEN'S SONG

This might seem to some like far too much to ask. What power could there be in willing suffering, in willing loss, in willing death? And who would be willing to pay such a price? The early Christians were willing to pay it, for one simple reason:

they had encountered Jesus on the other side of death. Here was the proof: there was a grave-cracking, evil-shattering power loose in the world. Jesus said that all who joined him in the practice of this costly power would join him for its priceless victory. They believed him.

The book of Revelation records the lyrics of a stunning hymn, constantly on replay in the court of heaven:

> Now the salvation and power and kingdom of our God,
>   and the authority of his Christ have come.
> The accuser of our brothers and sisters,
>   who accuses them day and night before our God,
>   has been thrown down.
> They gained the victory over him on account of the blood
>   of the Lamb
>   and the word of their witness.
> Love for their own lives didn't make them afraid to die.
> (Revelation 12:10–11)

"Accuser" is a literal translation of the word *Satan*. The song celebrates the ultimate defeat of evil, of all that has resisted the goodness and justice of God. According to heaven's song, there are two ways that ordinary people come to participate in the triumph of heaven: Through the activity of Jesus, who willingly surrendered his own life. And through their willingness to mingle their own lives and bodies with his, in a voluntary offering of love.

This is the power that turns history. This is the only power that will bring heaven home to earth.

THE END OF CHRISTENDOM

After sixteen hundred years of Christendom, Christianity is losing its dominance, its default status in much of the West. The church has less and less control over culture or government. Jesus followers have begun to look strange to their neighbors again. Some are responding to this moment by fighting as hard as possible to regain seats of power. But perhaps we might view this moment instead as a God-given window of opportunity.

Jesus followers have a chance at this critical time to repent—to reject the alliance with Satan and his methods by which we have gained the world at deep cost to all our souls. We have a chance to cut the head off evil's Trojan horse. We have a chance to rediscover the revolutionary new form of power that Jesus revealed—a kind of power that works *with* the grain of God's kingdom instead of against it.

This is our moment to rediscover the power of prayer. The world is trying desperately to combat evil with guns and armies. This is like trying to saw steel with a plastic butter knife or put out fire using gas; it is an effort doomed at best to fail and at worst to tragically backfire. Such weapons are ill-suited to the nature of the opponent. Prayer is a laser, honed to cut to the very heart of evil. It is one of the few weapons that can even get to the field where the core battle is being fought. And Jesus followers are uniquely equipped to wield it. There is no greater gift we could offer the world.

Prayer doesn't invoke God—God is already aware and present and engaged. Prayer doesn't control God—God isn't waiting for our instructions to know what to do. But through prayer we can open wide the door to the world and consent on behalf of humanity and creation to God's delivering power, rising from beneath us. Prayer is part of our God-given say-so as small image-bearers in creation, our chance to affect the course of history by aligning our own yes with God's.

This is our moment to rediscover the power of courageous witness. Witness is not a fearful silence where we cannot disagree or where we hide the truth we know for fear of causing offense. Witness is also not verbal combat where we fly around picking fights or shouting others down. Witness is open, vulnerable testimony to what we have seen, heard, touched, and tasted. It is a humble, risky, completely free offering of the best of what we understand. It is a gift made without demand or expectation of return. It is a gift extended with full preparation to absorb the cost of either acceptance or rejection.

The power of witness reveals the high stakes of truthfulness within the community of Jesus. If Jesus' people cannot be trusted to speak the truth in the small things, there is no reason on earth anyone should trust us for truth in the large ones. Witness is a form of power that depends in significant part on the integrity, the reliability, of the vessel carrying it.

Above all this, this is our moment to rediscover the power of the cross—the power of self-sacrificial, suffering love. The cross on a church building or necklace is anything but a benign symbol. It is the sign of a revolution. It is a proclamation of the counterintuitive shape of the power that overcomes evil and sets the world right. In the war for the world, Jesus is recruiting an army that will lay down Satan's weapons, the power of *over*, and will fight with the power of *under*, the evil-shattering power of God.

The power of returning curse with blessing. The power of suffering instead of inflicting it. The power of willing sacrifice. The power of lives surrendered for love of enemies who are still in evil's thrall. To exercise this kind of power is to become like Jesus, the very image of God. It's to become a partner with God in the global rescue story. The church has spent far too long playing the game on Satan's terms. The time has come to engage the war on Jesus' terms. History belongs to the Lamb who was slain. And to ordinary people who take up their cross and follow him.

That cracking? It's the sound of Satan's scepter breaking. It's the sound of heaven splitting open.

Behold, evil and all of creation, the world-remaking Power of Beneath.

CONVERSATION STARTERS

1. How do you think humans normally define power? Where is this kind of "worldly" power effective, and where is it not?
2. How does Jesus redefine popular notions of power?
3. Why do you think Jesus' redefinition of power, so clear to the early church, was overlooked for so much of Christian history?
4. What practical questions or dilemmas do you struggle with in contemplating what it would mean to shift your practice of power to align with Jesus'?
5. How do you think the three tools of God-styled power (bold prayer, courageous witness, self-sacrificial love) could be applied and practiced in twenty-first-century contexts?

8

Fault Lines

A Different Way to Disagree

DILEMMA

CONFLICTED MOVEMENTS

If there's one overarching feature that defines our time, it's *conflict*. Conflict between nations. Conflict between neighbors. Conflict in society. Conflict in the church. Conflict within families. We're not talking here about conflicts of the everyday variety, like the neighborhood spat over the pet rooster who loses his mind at four in the morning, or the shouting match that ensues when someone eats somebody else's leftover orange chicken (true stories both). We're talking about what's been described as "high conflict"[1]—the kind of conflict that feels all-encompassing, life or death, good versus evil.

Chasms seem to be opening up—giant rifts that divide sibling from sibling, neighbor from neighbor, community from community. It feels like half the people around us have

---

1. Amanda Ripley, *High Conflict: How We Get Trapped and How We Get Out* (New York: Simon and Schuster, 2021).

suddenly started speaking a foreign moral language we can't make heads or tails of. We're baffled how others could be so ignorant, or so naïve. Clashes are public and emotional. Some of the conflicts feel downright existential, a threat to our very being. Sometimes, truth be told, we just feel viscerally disgusted by each other's aesthetics.

"High conflicts" are unfolding across all Western culture. But no question, they are burning especially hot within the Jesus movement. Local communities of Jesus followers who have worshiped side by side for years are looking at each other side-eyed with growing unease, wondering if the guy across the aisle has met Jesus at all. Institutions of learning and parachurch ministries find themselves caught in a tightening vise between constituencies with contradictory demands. Denominations are ripping apart with messy, jagged edges, as family members furiously cling to opposite sides of the gash. The church resembles a melting Arctic glacier, breaking apart chunk by chunk, each new split apparently speeding up the dissolution of the whole.

To be fair, conflict isn't exactly new within the Jesus movement. Five hundred years ago, during the last reformation, a major break occurred in the church between those embracing a radical rethink (who became known as Protest-ants) and those whose significant concerns about the movement gave them pause. But the divisions didn't stop there. Differences emerged between the protesters themselves. Reformers agreed on some ideas, such as the centrality of scriptural authority. Yet other matters, like the nature of communion or the use of religious images, were fiercely disputed. Factions clustered around leaders. Verbal debates devolved into imprisonments, exiles, and executions.

One faction of protesters, known as Anabaptists ("re-baptizers"), came to the startling conclusion that killing your enemies was not, perhaps, what Jesus had in mind when he commanded loving them. However, despite this apparent spiritual breakthrough, the Anabaptists, too, spent subsequent centuries compulsively dividing into factions as group after group failed to live up to each other's expectations of what following Jesus required.

The last reformation recalibrated and revitalized Christian faith in vital ways. But in the haste to dispose of dirty ecclesial bathwater, sometimes precious things were thrown away. Factions of Jesus followers reacted against each other's errors, overcompensating in ways that pushed both toward less nuanced positions. Over time, the distinction between splitting logs and splitting hairs got lost in fog. Centuries later, we find ourselves in a world with forty-five thousand Christian denominations—and divisions still multiplying exponentially. With this legacy of the last reformation in mind, it wouldn't be surprising if some hear talk of a *new* reformation moment and think, "Great. Just what the world needs—more splinter groups of Christians convinced that they own Jesus . . . or at least the first-class cabin on Rapture Air."

DRIVERS OF FACTIONALISM

Similar dynamics of factionalism also plague nonreligious social and activist movements. Energy builds around an idea that seems obviously good to many—let's say, publicly funded treats for dogs (who are, after all, humanity's last defense against total psychological breakdown). But then pro-dog groups develop additional orthodoxies—all treats must be bone-shaped, or flavored like cheese, or there should be no treats for dogs without treats for cats too. Friction grows. Some individuals advocate for only vegan treat ingredients. Others respond with blogposts accusing the vegans of cruelty to animals. If enough people take their side, the movement splits in two—usually losing significant momentum in the process.

The questions involved here are real and can't be treated lightly. How much do we need to agree on to cooperate? What do we do with our differences? What, if anything, should be disqualifying for membership in a movement? After all, a group with no shared center at all has no reason to exist, and for people to be safe, there must be rules to the game. Football is a different affair if everyone gets to play with their own preferred ball-shape. Ditto if you erase the sidelines and let players chase through the stands.

Culturally, we have also begun grappling with the concept of complicity—the idea that our silence, our tolerance, our passivity, our uncritical association can contribute to major wrongs. This realization has been a costly lesson of history. Racism, harassment and abuse, even genocide have occurred not just because a few people were terribly wicked but because many more stood by, didn't wish to stir the pot, didn't want to deal with conflict or lost status or jobs.

The trouble is, there are just so many important things about which people and groups can be wrong. It can be genuinely challenging to know who is getting *enough* right. Our fiercest conflicts often involve people with whom we share the most in common . . . because they're the ones who we believe should know better, gosh darn it. Disagreement frequently feels far more threatening when it comes from within our own movement. If we have to face a bear, most of us would just as soon have that bear be *outside* the car we're trying to drive.

Factionalism is a challenging problem to solve on any front, and the stakes rarely feel higher than when it comes to religion or politics—which is probably why these areas tend to provoke the most intractable divisions. Therefore any potential

Christian reform movement will inevitably confront its own particular version of the urgent questions that beset all such movements: Can the Jesus movement be re-formed without creating fifty thousand new splinter groups, each convinced that all the others are full of heretics and witches? Can the bathwater be purified without losing any more babies? Can we argue without driving each other into reactive corners? Can we disagree with our allies without turning into a clown car of fighting bears? Could we dare to dream of a new reformation, one with real integrity, that doesn't just *avoid* the factionalism of the previous one but could actually begin to *reverse* it? It is an audacious hope, for certain. But then again, Jesus never evoked any other kind.

FALSE SOLUTIONS

One thing is clear: we will not get where we need to be by treating our differing convictions as if they do not matter. You might hear this approach advocated—less explicitly, of course—by leaders trying to preserve established institutions. You might also hear it taken up by everyday people sick and tired of the bickering: "Can't we all just get along? The differences between us *aren't that big of a deal.*"

There are three significant problems with a sweep-it-under-the-rug strategy for managing disagreement. First, the decision to prioritize unity at all costs often ends up costing a group its identity or purpose. You're left with a room full of heavy metal drummers and prima ballerinas sitting on their hands because they can't agree on what to do with them. We all know institutions like this, held together by nothing but habit or fear of a messy breakup. The primary mission of the organization becomes convincing everyone to stay in their chairs, to keep the lights on a little while longer. The result is almost always the same. People will tolerate this for a time, whether out of inertia or historical loyalty. But eventually they realize they no longer know why they're in this particular room, and they slip out the door one by one.

The second problem with this strategy is that it's frequently disingenuous. When people say "Our differences shouldn't divide us," what they often mean is *"These* differences shouldn't divide us." It's not that they really don't have any lines in the sand or don't believe that some questions are defining. It's just that they don't care much about the specific line that's important to their neighbor.

The third problem with unity at all costs is that it functionally favors the status quo. Existing structures of power or control end up locked in place, because nothing is permitted to raise a significant challenge. Such a status quo bias presumes that radical disruption and course-correction is never needed—let alone demanded by the Spirit of God.

There's no point in joining a movement without meaning. Some differences really do matter, and we don't always agree on which ones. These are the realities we must navigate as we seek a way to hold convictions that doesn't leave us all impaled on the ten-foot-pole we prefer to keep between us and "them" (that is, the dreadfully wrong ones).

REDISCOVERY

THE CHARACTER OF TOGETHERNESS

Any movement purporting to pursue a better, more faithful Christian story has a responsibility to consider how it will relate to Jesus followers who have a different idea of what "better" and "more faithful" mean. Lucky for us, we aren't the first generation to confront this question. The early Christian community was no stranger to conflict and division. As the story of Jesus spread from Jewish farms and fishing villages to multicultural urban centers, values and intuitions often collided. Which festivals must be observed? How do you eat together if the content of your plates disgusts and offends each other? What exactly counts as a Jesus-shaped sexual ethic? Can women teach or not? The debate over circumcision reached such a fever pitch as to provoke a churchwide council (see Acts 15). Even issues apparently "resolved" in formal settings continued to evoke considerable debate in local communities on the ground.[2]

It's no coincidence that many letters preserved by the early church are profoundly concerned with questions of disagreement and unity within the nascent Christian community. This is particularly true of the letter to the Jesus followers at Ephesus.[3] Christian missionary Paul writes, "Conduct yourselves with all humility, gentleness, and patience. Accept each other with love, and make an effort to preserve the unity of the Spirit with the peace that ties you together" (Ephesians 4:2–3). Paul clearly suggests here that unity is going to take *work*. It will be possible only if members of this community cultivate specific habits of heart and mind that are indispensable to cohesion across difference.

---

2. See Colossians 2:16–23; 1 Corinthians 6:12–9:27; Romans 14:1–15:13 for examples of the kinds of conflicts being negotiated in the early church.

3. It is potentially telling that the earliest manuscripts of this letter lack the traditional "address label" at the opening that names the person or community to whom the letter is being sent. This could indicate that the letter now known as Ephesians was being copied and resent to a variety of churches who were all facing similar dilemmas of division and unity.

Conduct yourselves with humility. Humility is the concession we owe reality. Billions of people have lived before us. Many have held quite different beliefs about God and the world. A lot of these people were and are sincere Jesus followers. The odds that you and your buddy Dave had a metaphysical breakthrough after that second drink and were the first to accurately decode the entire cosmic map of Reality seem objectively pretty low. You and I and Dave are probably all very wrong about something. We just don't yet know what.

There's a proper humility that belongs to working with live electrical wires. So, too, working with the Spirit of God. There's power here to transform, to light up the night, to charge up the paddles that jump-start a new heart. But handled without due humility and respect, that same heart-starting power can roast your neighbor's liver like a rotisserie chicken. We owe it to ourselves, each other, and most of all to truth to acknowledge the inconceivable vastness of what we are touching when we seek out God. Humility is not an absence of strong convictions; it is an acknowledgement that we are cracked teacups trying to contain an Ocean.

Conduct yourselves with gentleness. Gentleness was a virtue lauded by the ancients that rarely appears in modern discourse, perhaps because of a misperception of its meaning. Gentleness is not glorified weakness, nor is it a term for those whose fight-or-flight instinct is permanently stuck on play-dead possum mode. Precisely the opposite. Gentleness is the discipline of power under control. It's Superman picking up a champagne flute without crushing it to sand.

Jesus didn't forbid his followers power; he assumed that they would have it. The question for Jesus was always how power should be exercised. As we saw in the previous chapter, the power that Jesus taught and modeled was never directed toward kicking out knees or swinging swords at necks. It was a power that lifted others from underneath. A power that bore other peoples' weight and carried others' burdens. Gentleness is power so thoroughly under control of its bearer that it can cut straight through armor of lies or shackles of prejudice without slicing open the fragile human veins underneath.

Conduct yourselves with patience. Patience is the holy habit of taking the long view. No one hates this concept more than modern people who check the shipping status of packages they ordered an hour ago and shake their fist when the website takes three seconds to load. If something is wrong, we want it fixed yesterday. But as Paul points out elsewhere, it is the kindness and patience of God that leads people to change (Romans 2:4)—not the probably very real impulse to rigorously shake them upside-down like a clogged ketchup bottle.

We often imagine righteousness (right living) as a race where some pull far ahead while others meander behind. We want to sic a pit bull on the sluggards—not to hurt them, mind you, just to scare them into picking up the pace a bit. However, life is far more complicated than a single-track race. We are all running many races at once. In some we're miles ahead. In others we're barely limping along. In some we've lost the road completely and are slogging through ditch weeds.

Jesus invites his community into a habit of long-suffering and daily "gracing" that is grounded in the recognition of our common struggle. Someone limping from a sprain will not run faster simply because we loose the dogs. What they may require in order to keep advancing is someone else who slows their own natural pace to lend a shoulder of support. Perhaps, at least sometimes, the speed of the race may be less important than helping each other keep moving forward.

THE CENTER OF GRAVITY

The habits of character just named comprise a critical foundation for any community that hopes to bear disagreement without endless fracturing. But this is only the beginning. As we've
noted, for a movement to remain viable and transformative as
a movement, it requires a shared center, a common core gener-
ating the gravity that draws and holds the movement together.

This need for a shared center was very clearly on the minds
of leaders in the early Jesus movement. Paul writes to the Jesus
followers in Ephesus, "We aren't supposed to be infants any
longer who can be tossed and blown about by every wind that
comes from teaching with deceitful scheming and the tricks
people play to deliberately mislead others" (Ephesians 4:14).
The early church was constantly alert to the real possibility
that its identity could be overtaken, reinscribed, by alternative
ideologies and agendas. Every culture has its own zeitgeist, its
own totalizing energy, that runs beneath the surface of the era
like a riptide. It would be easy, so easy, for the unwary to be
pulled into a different sea without even recognizing it. The last
thing the world needs from the church is just another group
spouting fad philosophy or tattooing on new eyebrows every
time the fashions change.

Against this condition, Paul proposes an alternative: "By
speaking the truth with love, let's grow in every way into
Christ, who is the head. The whole body grows from him, as
it is joined and held together by all the supporting ligaments"
(Ephesians 4:15–16). Paul identifies the gravitational core of
the Christian movement in a single word: Christ. He is the
anchor that keeps the movement from drifting. More than
that, he is the Sea in which the church is given the freedom
to sail. He is the soil from which all true life grows. He is the
Sun whom the planets orbit, the center of gravity that holds

the solar system together. The Christian movement has always been defined by relationship to a living person and the historical events of his life, death, and resurrection.

REDISCOVERY #8:

The unity of the church is secured by the center it orbits.

In a broader sense, early Jesus followers often referred to their shared center as "the kerygma," which means "the preaching." This was a shorthand term for the core discoveries emergent from Jesus that had ignited the Christian movement. The content of this core is visible and consistent in their earliest sermons and letters: Jesus was God's "authorized representative"—a fact made unmistakably clear when God raised him from the dead. Jesus died to save the world from sin and the hell that it unleashes. Jesus is Lord, calling all to allegiance and a new way of being together in the world. Jesus has sent the Spirit, God's presence among us to speak and empower and transform. From day one, this was the central story around which the Jesus movement revolved.

Not all listeners to Jesus heard his teachings exactly the same way. The collection of early Christian writings known as the New Testament contains four gospels. Each account of Jesus' words is compiled by a different person, writing for a different community. These writers highlight different themes, sometimes hearing the emphases of Jesus' stories differently or applying them in different ways. James and Paul, both highly committed, respected followers of Jesus who have letters preserved in the New Testament, have such different ways of talking about what faith in Jesus means that some—including, infamously, the sixteenth-century reformer Martin Luther—have not been able to bear the tension and suggested one must go. However, this variation was embraced by the early Christian church, understood to exist within the unified field of one common kerygma.

Other cases, however, were treated differently. Some people, for example, claimed that Jesus had imparted secret revelation to a few elites. Some claimed that Jesus had no real physical body. Here the early Christian recognized a crucial distinction. Storytellers like Matthew and John, James and Jude and Paul, were tracing different orbits but circling a common center of gravity. Other storytellers were orbiting different stars, recognizably distinct kerygmas.

A central reason why the church was moved to develop a canon of authoritative texts (that is, the Christian New Testament) was to help distinguish variation that orbited a common kerygma from that which represented a separate solar system. Some teachers were faithfully in conversation with the historical Jesus to whom the earliest witnesses testified. Others were circling alternative philosophies and authorities.

The unity of the early Christian movement did not require every person or community to trace exactly the same orbit, to have the same favored metaphor for describing how Jesus saves or exactly the same understanding of how his teachings on money applied. It did, however, require that they orbit a common Sun—the incarnate Son of God on a mission to save, not a few but the entire world. Unity could encompass many differences, even passionate disagreements, but there was a time to acknowledge when core narratives had parted ways so completely that the motion of groups was being directed by different suns.

CHARTING THE DARTBOARD

Everyone, of course, would very much like to know how to tell when this point has been reached. Anyone who claims to possess a mathematical formula for an objective, indisputable answer is, frankly, selling magic beans. But there are strategies we might use for making wiser and less reactive judgments.

Some have suggested imagining Christian faith (or any other belief set) like a dartboard, a series of concentric circles with a bull's-eye in the middle. Specific convictions fall in different rings across the board. A few lie in the bull's-eye center—for example, "Jesus died for sin" or "Jesus is Lord," core tenets around which the early Christian movement formed, the heart of the kerygma. Perhaps on the second ring out we might pin our explanations of *how* Jesus' death for sin was accomplished—a very important question, but not quite as fundamental as the accomplishment itself. Our beliefs about the best prayer techniques or church governance structures we might locate on the outer ring.

These are of course judgment calls. Many people will passionately disagree about the coordinates of many convictions. For this reason, in constructing our dartboard, the best approach is probably to start with the bull's-eye and work our way out.

At the bull's-eye we consider what is definitional to Christianity—the core energy fueling the movement, the heart of the story, the foundational discoveries on which the house is built. For inner rings, we consider what is clearest, most explicit, what is most widely recognized and embraced by communities of Jesus discerning the Spirit across time and geography.

As we move outward, we weigh what matters might possibly fall within the characterization of "disputable." This category of conviction is proposed by the apostle Paul himself in response to some of the conflicts besetting the early church (Romans 14:1). These are questions on which evidence may conflict. Matters about which we might have a passionately discerned opinion but not directions that come explicitly from the lips of Jesus. Issues on which Jesus followers sincerely seeking truth might disagree without forsaking the kerygma.

In his writing, Paul makes a distinction between "the Lord's command"—on, for example, a subject like divorce, which Jesus addressed explicitly (see 1 Corinthians 7:10)—and Paul's own counsel on a subject like interreligious marriage, which involves an extension of principle or judgment he makes as a trustworthy person who is full of the Spirit of God (see 1 Corinthians 7:25, 40). The latter is not unimportant, nor does it lack authority. But it is also not kerygma and is recognized as requiring a level of inference that distinguishes it from Jesus' direct instructions.

To name a conviction as part of an outer ring on the dartboard does not imply that it is unimportant or without significant implications. It is simply to acknowledge that such a belief is dependent on even more fundamental convictions (inner rings) that may be shared by other Jesus followers with a different outer-ring conviction or practice. The act of communion as a sharing in Jesus' self-giving is more fundamental than the frequency, the liturgy, or fermentation of the grapes. No matter where on the dartboard you locate your specific definitions of sexual ethics, the conviction that a Christian's body is "not their own" and is meant to be fully submitted to Jesus (1 Corinthians 6:19) lies one ring deeper in. The former convictions are built on the foundation of the latter.

Keep in mind the key principle of dartboard design: proportionality. If everything is bull's-eye, there's hardly a point. Not everything can be kerygma. If every dispute is perceived to threaten the center, splinter groups will multiply into infinity as each disagreement necessitates starting a new board. The logical long-term outcome of such a practice in an individualistic culture is billions of people playing darts all alone.

WHY AND HOW TO DIVIDE

Once a person or group has mapped out their dartboard, they might wonder what exactly to do with it in practice. One key purpose of dartboard-mapping is to ensure that our motion-detecting alarm isn't constantly set off by moths. Deliberately mapping our dartboard allows us to recalibrate our threat detector. It keeps us from perceiving every person or group who disagrees with us as a bus that is running roughshod right over Jesus. Taking the time to notice how much is shared (or not) in our deeper rings provides a much better starting point from which to discuss the reasons for our significant differences.

Another important use of our dartboard map is to help us find more partners in mission. Identifying and placing increased importance on our core allows us to cooperate with others on projects that serve that shared center. We can acknowledge real differences on outer rings and the consequences of those differences without losing sight of common interests and purpose. Missional partnerships do not always have to encompass the entire dartboards. Valuable partners may be recognized in different combinations of rings.

There are also legitimate reasons for groups to separate when it becomes apparent they are operating with different bull's-eyes or even different outer rings. There is no "rule" for exactly how much must be shared in order to cooperate. The decision will often be affected by a group's specific mission. Mission goes awry when the people working together are aiming at different targets, flinging their darts crossways with each other. Some forms of mission may require that only the bull's-eye be in common. Other forms of mission directly implicate the outer rings. The important thing to keep in mind is that it is possible to recognize that missions have diverged without lighting anyone else's dartboard on fire.

Paul reminds the Jesus followers at Ephesus to keep in mind the big picture: "[God's] purpose was to equip God's people for the work of serving and building up the body of Christ until we all reach the unity of faith and knowledge of God's Son. God's goal is for us to become mature adults—to be fully grown, measured by the standard of the fullness of Christ" (Ephesians 4:12–13). We are all, according to Paul, still on a learning journey. We are growing in knowledge of Jesus and comprehension of his ways. We are growing up into his stature, into his character. We're all in that ungainly teenage phase of stumbling over our own too-big feet.

Understanding the process of growth, we can look at each other and recognize in these awkward, pimply, half-grown siblings the signs of family resemblance, even when it's immature. Without compromising our center of gravity, we can acknowledge the existence of other planets, farther out perhaps (at least in our opinion) but still orbiting the same vast Sun.

Far from silencing our disagreements, this mutual recognition allows them to be voiced more fully. We grow "by speaking the truth with love," Paul says (Ephesians 4:15). The shared sun is our center. But planets, too, have gravity of their own that exerts a pull on each other. Our orbits around the Sun can be influenced by each other. The push and pull of honest, faithful disagreement is how Christian growth often occurs.

For those who seem to have diverged from our solar system entirely, we maintain both clear, shrewd vision and relentless hope. Two thousand years of Christian experience has earned us this. Even what seems to be lost may yet be drawn back around. Sometimes orbits are very long, but divine gravity is powerful, the most powerful thing that exists. We live in hope for each other.

TRANSFORMATION

THE TRAJECTORY PRINCIPLE

Imagine Jesus standing in the middle of a gymnasium. Just a few feet away from him stands your classic "good person." She drives a minivan. She never misses church. She shouts things like "Fudge nugget!" and "Son of a brisket!" when she is really mad. Across the gym in the farthest corner is a guy who is, to put it frankly, a real mess. His son and daughter haven't spoken to him in years. His trash is full of (unrecycled!) beer cans. He hasn't washed his sheets in months. His prayers are mostly one-word sentences like "Help!" and "Please!"

Question: Which one of these people is on God's team?

The religious leaders in Jesus' day had a clear answer: the person on God's team was the one who followed the rules, who did the most things right. Meaning them, of course. They were the ones who counted steps on Sabbath to be sure "walking" wasn't "working." They were the ones who gave up eating several days a week to free their mouths for more elaborate prayers.

Yet Jesus spent much of his time with prostitutes and tax cheats. He claimed that occupying soldiers and small-town screwups were closer to God than many pastors and priests.

More than that, he implied that some of the "best" people anyone knew actually belonged to God's opposition. What gives?
What possible yardstick could Jesus be using to measure that
leads him to count the town drunk in and the pastor with the
ten-pound study Bible out? Many, even most, people listening
to Jesus, could not make heads or tails of it.

The unexpected answer is that Jesus was not using any
measuring stick at all. Jesus did not identify God's team by
proximity or distance. The revolutionary truth the religious
experts could not imagine was that Jesus was identifying his
team not by position in space but by *trajectory of motion*.[4]

These "sinners" were far from God. They had judged so
many things wrong. They had made a series of choices that
got them in way over their heads. They had hurt themselves
and others. They were lonely. They were desperate. When
Jesus showed up, shining with mercy, they were drawn to him
inexorably. Their faces tracked his motion, as flowers track the
sun. They followed him wherever he went.

Many of the "righteous," on the other hand, were busy
doing the right things but for all the wrong reasons. They were
good for the side benefits. They were generous for the returns.
They followed the rules but neglected the love. Their prayers
were self-justifying speeches, not appeals to the unmerited
goodness of God. They were nearer to Jesus in body than
almost anybody else. But they were not following him. In fact,
they were facing in the opposite direction.

Jesus did not appear to hold moral perfection as his
standard for association. The opposite, in fact. He accepted
the reputational blowback of friendship with people others

---

4. Mark Baker describes the practical difference between "positional" and "directional"
models of church in his book *Centered-Set Church: Discipleship and Community without
Judgmentalism* (Downers Grove: InterVarsity Press, 2021).

considered out of bounds. He was who he was. He spoke what was true. He didn't hide his thoughts or beliefs. But he showed up for everyone—gluttons and drunkards, religious hypocrites, prostitutes and adulterers, self-righteous punks. Jesus was, by intentional practice, an indiscriminate dinner guest. He treated the relational dinner table as the most likely context for transformation.

And when it came time to judge who was with him and who was against, as sometimes is required, Jesus didn't create a spreadsheet for computing an individual's overall behavior or theological rightness. He looked for movement. He looked for trajectory. He looked for what, or whom, they were facing. He looked for people who were humble and hungry and reaching and stumbling and even face-planting in the direction of divine grace.

Imagine a movement defined not by where people are but by whom and what they are seeking. Imagine belonging defined not by a point in space but by directional movement across time. This is the glorious chaos of Jesus' imagination. Any movement that is his will have the same character: definition not by the outer boundaries but by relationship to its brilliant, burning center.

THE SOURCE OF UNITY

One of the core rediscoveries of the last reformation was that salvation is through faith.

To many, "faith" came to be understood as "believing the right things." By logical extension, Christian unity must then be rooted in our shared right thinking or abstract belief. We belong together with people who think the same way we do.

This "intellectualization" of identity is one of the powerful forces fueling polarization across Western cultures. Our people, we imagine, must surely be those who see the world as we do—which, coincidentally, is most often those who share our class, race, education, and background. It's hard to conceive of a strong connective force that's not rooted in either the ancient tribal system of blood ties or the modern tribal system of intellectual assent and ideology.

But the unity of the early church was not rooted in the intellect. The early Jesus followers believed that salvation was through faith, and faith meant an active, trusting reliance. Faith was trust in One who loved us when we were unlovable, when we were wrong about every conceivable question. Faith was reliance on One who rescues us, forgives us, gifts us, and transforms us. This is the source of Christian unity. Our unity is rooted in the common Voice that summons us. The common Hand that heals us. The common Grace that holds us. We are bound together by his common choice of us all.

This is what Paul attempts to make clear to the diverse Jesus followers in the city of Ephesus:

> Accept each other with love, and make an effort to preserve the unity of the Spirit with the peace that ties you together. You are one body and one spirit, just as God also called you in one hope. There is one Lord, one faith, one baptism, and one God and Father of all, who is over all, through all, and in all. (Ephesians 4:2–6)

This is Paul, defining the center.

The unity of the center can and must be actively preserved. But it does not have to be created or achieved. It's not something we build or make happen. It's the default state of a solar system with one Lord, one Spirit, one source of gravity holding us in orbit, making us what we are. Our unity is secured by the common center itself. Venus, Paul seems to say, stop wasting your time trying to veto Pluto's planetary membership, and focus on bending around the Sun!

This is what this final rediscovery is really about. It's an acknowledgment that unity isn't truly ours to achieve. It is *given* by the common center. In an age of endless fracturing, when the distance between groups seems increasingly vast, to belong to Jesus is to become part of a universe of people who think quite differently from us but who are still bound by relationship to the same blazing star—and who are being changed over time by that common binding.

The Spirit is constantly working to draw things into tighter orbit around Jesus. In the end, perhaps all eight rediscoveries are just many ways of saying that one thing: Jesus. Jesus. Jesus. Jesus as the universe's fundamental logic. Jesus as history's ultimate trajectory. Jesus as the perfect revelation of God. Jesus as the perfect image of humanity. Jesus the author. Jesus the rescuer. Jesus at the beginning of time, and Jesus at the end. Jesus at the center of everything. Jesus.

A CALL TO ACTION

The last Christian reformation generated desperately needed course corrections but also resulted in centuries of inter-Christian conflict and sectarian fracturing. During the next reformation, whenever it might come, we have a chance to chart a different course. There is a way of defining Christian identity and potential for cooperative mission that is rooted in a common center and not the disputed border ground. This unexpected source of unity in an age of polarization may be one of the most defining features of Christian witness, the taste of a truly different world that Jesus Christ makes possible.

In an age of pluralism, no one has yet cracked the code for how to be together in a way that neither papers over disagreements nor allows them to own the whole story. Few things could be more revolutionary than a community that refuses to allow conflict to diminish each other's humanity. Few things could be more transformational than a community that devotes less energy to policing its borders and more to elevating and celebrating its glorious center of gravity.

What would it take for the church to adopt this posture? Such a shift depends on an ever-growing trust that the One who set this universe in motion has ordered all things toward himself. It depends on trust that the One who started this story is able to finish it. It depends on trust that the gravity of grace will ultimately do its job.

My brothers and sisters, whoever you are, we may agree or disagree on our dreams for the future of the Jesus movement, on our identification of its most urgent problems or most promising solutions. But here's one thing I know for certain— Jesus adores you. So let me make a modest proposal: let's let this be the starting place for how we think of each other, speak to each other, speak about each other—as people adored by Jesus. Until we all reach the unity of faith and knowledge of God's Son. Until we all become fully grown adults, measured by the standard of Christ. Until Divine Gravity draws us all straight into its burning heart.

CONVERSATION STARTERS

1. What do you think is the bull's-eye center of the Christian movement? Why do you think so?

2. How does this approach to disagreement sound different from the church's recent history? How does it differ from common cultural ways of treating disagreement?

3. Do you think you can be in close relationship with someone who is wrong about something important without being complicit in their wrongs? Explain your answer in light of Jesus.
4. What would change if you valued trajectory over position? Whom or what might you see differently?
5. What part of this vision for unity do you find the most challenging to accept or to live out?

Conclusion

WAITING BY THE TOMB

Jesus' friend Lazarus has fallen ill. Jesus is unworried. "This illness isn't fatal," he tells his disciples. "It's for the glory of God so that God's Son can be glorified through it" (John 11:4). Then Lazarus dies, provoking some serious questions about Jesus' credibility. Martha, sister of the dead, believes that Jesus has power to turn things around even now. But when Jesus orders, "Roll back the gravestone," even faithful Martha has second thoughts. Whatever comes out of this tomb, she thinks, is sure to smell like the bowels of hell.

Christianity has fallen ill. Some would argue fatally. Even Jesus followers might reasonably have their share of doubts. If Jesus were really who he claims, would things have gotten this bad? And even if the story doesn't end here, will we really want whatever comes out of the tomb? After so much rot, maybe some things are better left buried.

It's comforting to know that we're not the first to have such complicated feelings. Generations before us have gone through periods when it seemed all the sacred mountains were falling, but after two thousand years, the church still stands.

That's the thing about traveling with Jesus—you never know for sure what's a tomb and what's a chrysalis, what's really dead and what's just counting down to its rebirthday. Nothing is truly over until Jesus says it's over. Maybe this present illness is fatal. Or maybe it's not after all. Maybe it's for the glory of God so God's Son can be glorified through it.

Resurrection is a gift of God, not an achievement of human effort. It's not something we can conjure or produce. But it is something we can watch for, waiting by the tomb with our honest mixture of hope and doubts. Those who linger might just get a chance to help unwind the graveclothes and be among the first to glimpse the shape emerging from beneath.

AN EMERGING MOVEMENT

In this book we've explored eight rediscoveries that could mark a desperately needed re-formation of Christianity in the twenty-first century:

1. Jesus is the authoritative lens through which God is seen and the Bible is interpreted.
2. Salvation encompasses the setting right of all things, on earth as it is in heaven.
3. A Christian is one who acknowledges Jesus as Lord and follows him in life and death.
4. A new community is both the means and goal of God's transformational activity.
5. Jesus' people are sent as ambassadors for God's reconciling work.
6. The Spirit guides and resources God's mission.
7. Evil is overcome by the power of sacrificial love.
8. The unity of the church is secured by the center it orbits.

These rediscoveries are not my own invention, nor do they represent some modern innovation. They are course corrections that orient the church back toward the heart of the most ancient Christian story. And they are presently being rediscovered in varying orders and combinations by Jesus followers from diverse traditions all over the world.

Christians in Ghana are finding how the health-and-wealth gospel is overturned when the Bible is interpreted through the lens of Jesus. Churches in the United States are repenting of their alliance with unholy power. Christians in India are glimpsing how a faith defined by its center can create new possibilities for unity in diversity. Churches in post-Christian Europe are rediscovering the power of sacrificial service as a form of prophetic witness. Christians in Australia are learning how the Spirit's voice is clarified when tested by the character of Jesus.

These rediscoveries are occurring spontaneously in many places at once. The movement is structurally decentralized yet seemingly responding to a common, unseen pull. The gravity of grace is working, drawing the church around Jesus again.

Many have asked whether this movement has a name. To my knowledge, no shorthand term has yet emerged. What we call it, how we categorize it, is far less important than what it is—a renewed commitment to match our stride with Jesus' and to come to know God, ourselves, and reality as we come to better know him.

The early Christians referred to themselves as "followers of the Way." The world has perhaps had enough of Christianity the Idea. Centuries of power abuses have inoculated much of Western culture against big rhetoric. But Christianity the Way is something else entirely. Never has a time been riper for a reimagined, communal embodiment of God-breathed

humanness and Jesus-shaped divinity—a Way of gratitude
and sacrifice, of integrity and enemy love, of generosity and
non-anxiety, of presence and awe-filled mystery.

THE QUESTION OF PRACTICE

This book has been full of big ideas. But talk alone won't fix
what has been broken. The early church rocked the world in
two primary ways: by embodying a radical existence of love
that offered hope for a better future, and by midwifing personal encounters with a living God.

God's plan has never been redemption by rhetoric. We are
saved because the Word became flesh. For this salvation to be
received, for it to work its way into the fiber of the world, it
must be enfleshed again in each generation by the people of
Jesus. This is why Jesus sent the Spirit, empowering his body
(the church) to become a living dwelling place of God.

The crucial question that remains is what these rediscoveries of the outline of God's rescue plan might look like in
embodied practice. In much of the West, Christianity currently has a bad reputation, one that it has largely earned. If
we believe that Jesus has something better to offer than the
deathly status quo, it is our God-entrusted role to proclaim
with our bodies a more beautiful alternative. This is a project
worth loosing our redeemed imaginations upon.

In my own small corner of the world, I see signs of it being
worked out. I've been in the room with communities defy-
ing the odds of polarization, actually hearing each other and
repenting of hasty judgments. I know people who've invited
homeless teenagers into their homes, offering tastes of a new
kind of family that Jesus makes possible. I've talked to churches
who've discovered that when they stopped fighting for power
and started caring for the poor, their neighbors suddenly got

curious again about what Jesus has to say. I've met people who are experiencing the power of the presence of the Spirit to heal deep-seated psychological trauma and free from bondage to addiction.

I can offer no comprehensive plan for embodied practice, because it will likely look different in each local setting. The Spirit excels at contextualization, at translating the gracious work of Jesus in each distinct culture and circumstance. It's the work of local communities of Jesus followers, listening to the Spirit, to discover what God's kingdom looks like planted in their local soil, to embody what Jesus looks like wearing their local clothes.

THE NEXT UNBINDING

I dream of seeing a church emerge from this period of tumult that looks somehow more like Jesus. And I want more than anything to be part of the work of communal unbinding. Perhaps you are with me. Maybe you feel the reformer's fire burning through you. Maybe you're ready to see Lazarus run. Perhaps you're eager to play your part in helping to unwrap the future.

If so, the time is now. I hope you will start conversations, ask deep questions, search for partners orbiting a radiant center. I hope you will *live*—boldly and generously, prayerfully and purposefully—in relationship with others. I pray you will be the movement you're longing to see. This movement isn't ours to control. But it is ours to embody in faithful response to the Spirit's nudging and in joyful anticipation of whatever may come next.

So come, my friends. I'll meet you at the tomb. Let's see for ourselves what God can do, what Jesus will call forth.

Acknowledgments

This book owes its existence in significant part to ongoing conversations within two communities.

The eight rediscoveries were first sketched on a hotel notepad at three in the morning after a late-night gathering of members of the Jesus Collective. The passion of this group for the future of the church, their desire to conform to Jesus, and their determination to get on board with whatever the Spirit is doing in our time renewed my hope and ignited my imagination. These conversations were critical in clarifying a fundamental question: "What might a Christian movement look like that recentered on Jesus?"

Members of the Jesus Collective Theology Circle were key dialogue partners in helping identify the shape of the movement and pain points to which it responds. I'm grateful to all the members of the group who shared their own hopes and insights: Shawna Boren, Greg Boyd, Adam Dyer, Paul Eddy, David Fitch, Leanne Friesen, Tania Harris, Hank Johnson, Edem Morny, Jonny Morrison, Samuel Sarpiya, and Levy Soko. Greg Boyd and Jon Hand with the Jesus Collective also both provided important feedback as early readers of the manuscript.

The second community that helped midwife this book into being was my own local congregation, Trinity Mennonite Church (Glendale, AZ). Their questions and comments in response to the sermon series "test run" of these ideas contributed significantly to the final result. Even more, their enthusiasm for the possibility of a "new reformation" and their stories about why it is urgently needed provided motivational fuel to keep the project moving forward at a difficult time. I'm particularly grateful to all those in my community who prayed me through the weeks of drafting and to the crew of incredible women who kept me fed so I could stay in the writing zone night after night.

Amy Gingerich at Herald Press had the vision for this book *as* a book after a seemingly divinely appointed airport taxi ride. Thanks to Laura Leonard and the rest of the team at Herald Press for believing in the project and shepherding it wisely.

I'm also grateful to my friend Scott Peterson, whose insights on Jesus' relationship with power shook me to my core and made me argue, wrestle, weep, repent, and ultimately marvel at the strange wisdom of God revealed in a cross. Having been humbled so thoroughly once, I'll never again read the Gospels without wondering what other wonders may be right in front of me, hidden by my blind spots, waiting for rediscovery. It's a terrifying and exhilarating experience. I wish it for everyone.

The Author

MEGHAN LARISSA GOOD is lead pastor at Trinity Mennonite Church in Glendale, Arizona. She has degrees from Gordon College, Duke Divinity School, and Portland Seminary. In addition to being a passionate preacher and storyteller, she is in demand as a speaker on biblical  hermeneutics, Anabaptism, and contemporary preaching. She is also the author of *The Bible Unwrapped: Making Sense of Scripture Today.*

Jesus Collective

About Jesus Collective

God is at work raising up a movement of churches, ministries, and disciples all around the world that are passionate about advancing a Jesus-centered, Jesus-looking kingdom.

This is a movement with roots in the Radical Reformation that welcomes Jesus followers from a wide range of backgrounds, traditions, and contexts. We place Jesus at the center of everything, choosing in our differences to unite around Christ in our increasingly post-Christian and polarized world.

Jesus Collective exists to amplify this movement, providing resources and relationship for those who choose to participate in more hopeful Jesus-centered expressions of faith.

In partnership with Herald Press, we are pleased to offer a line of books to fuel the Jesus-centered movement and provide vision for a more hopeful and relevant vision of Jesus in this cultural moment.

Learn more at JesusCollective.com.